Walk Me Into Heaven

Getting Ready for the Adventure of My Forever Life

Cindy Hamilton

Walk Me Into Heaven: Getting Ready for the Adventure of My Forever Life. Copyright 2023© Cindy Hamilton. All rights reserved. Printed in the United States of America. No part of this book may be used or reproduced in any manner whatsoever without written permission except in the case of brief quotations embodied in critical articles and reviews.

Unless otherwise indicated, all Scripture quotations are taken from the Holy Bible, New Living Translation, copyright © 1996, 2004, 2015 by Tyndale House Foundation. Used by permission of Tyndale House Publishers, Carol Stream, Illinois 60188. All rights reserved.

Scriptures taken from the Holy Bible, New International Version®, NIV®. Copyright © 1973, 1978, 1984, 2011 by Biblica, Inc.™ Used by permission of Zondervan. All rights reserved worldwide. www.zondervan.com The "NIV" and "New International Version" are trademarks registered in the United States Patent and Trademark Office by Biblica, Inc.™

"Scripture taken from THE MESSAGE. Copyright © 1993, 1994, 1995, 1996, 2000, 2001, 2002. Used by permission of NavPress Publishing Group."

Scriptures taken from The Amplified Bible ®. Copyright © 1954, 1958, 1962, 1964, 1965, 1987 Used by permission of The Lockman Foundation. All rights reserved.

Photo credits for cover: istock.com/588987856
Interior designed by Cindy Hamilton
ISBN: 9798398936568

*To my husband, Preston,
for 53 years and counting.
To my children and grandchildren:
You are why I
wrote this book.
To my precious friend, D'Arylan,
for being my encourager.
To Mrs. Ruby and Mrs. Lillie
for modeling grace and
courage to the end.*

Acknowledgments

The whole earth will acknowledge the Lord and return to him. All the families of the nations will bow down before him.
Psalm 22:27

Composing an acknowledgment page is always humbling. I am so grateful as I sit here and think about the people who have taken the time to read my manuscript and give feedback.

There have been several people who have generously helped me along the way with this book.

Special thanks to Sheryl, who used her English teacher's pen to carefully and kindly correct my manuscript. (Honestly!) Your encouragement helped me to move forward with this book.

Thank you, D'Arlyan. You are my Barnabas. Your enthusiasm is a blessing to me. Your spiritual feedback and insight are priceless.

Thank you to Preston—sitting outside the camper and reading through the manuscript. You probably would rather have been fishing. I love you.

Thank you to Martha. Cousin, you were so sweet to read through the book not one time but three times! That meant so much to me. None of this would have happened if it weren't for you 50+ years ago.

Thank you to my kids for reading through this book and giving their okay.

Thank you, Pastor Derek Smith. As my pastor, it meant so much that you sat down and listened to my heart. Thank you for taking the time to allow me to process my thoughts and ideas in this book.

"A great many persons imagine that anything said about heaven is only a matter of speculation. They talk about heaven much as they would about the air. Now there would not have been so much in Scripture on this subject if God had wanted to leave the human race in darkness about it."
–Author Dwight L. Moody, *Heaven*, 1900

Foreward

What happens when we die? We've all wondered about the process of leaving this world and slipping into eternity. Cindy Hamilton helps us explore the possibilities of the afterlife from a biblical perspective. You will go from the preparation and journey to your eternal home. Spending time thinking about eternity really matters, for what we think about eternity often reveals what we think of Jesus.

Let's face it: none of us like to contemplate our own mortality. However, the latest statistics show that 10/10 will die someday! We spend so much time trying to navigate this current life, while rarely training ourselves for the afterlife. Jesus said, "I go to prepare a place for you." If God is preparing a place for me, what will I do there? Will I be floating on clouds and playing a harp, or will I have responsibilities and purpose in Heaven?

Cindy uses her wit and humor to take you on a journey to the end. She will help you consider some of the most pressing concerns we keep locked away in the recesses of our minds. Questions like Does everyone go to Heaven? What will the New Jerusalem look like? Are my former pets in Heaven? And What is there to do in Heaven?

While using some hilarious examples and childhood memories, Cindy will cause you to ponder your own preparation for Heaven and your purpose on this earth. Take a moment and ask God to open your eyes of understanding as you embark on this adventure of considering your forever home.

Pastor Derek Smith, The Bridge Church,
Lonoke, Arkansas

x

Contents

The Preparation
Introduction 1
Before We Begin to Talk About Heaven 7
Getting Old is Heck (*or Not*) 15
The Courage to Get to the End. 25
College Hunks Hauling Junk (*or You Can't Take It With You*). 33

The Journey
Traveling Toward Heaven 43
The Spectators 53
The Hard Chapter (*or What Keeps You Out of Heaven*) 63
"Good News, Silas! You Were Right!" 73
Sore Puzzler (*or I'm So Confused*) 83

Home
Yearning To Be at Home With the Lord 95
"Look! I Am Making All Things New (*or a Fresh Start*) 103
Spending Forever Time With Jesus (*or the Best Part*) 111
The Holy City—The New Jerusalem 121
   (*or City Girl or Country Girl*)
I Can Only Imagine 131
What's There to Do Forever and Ever and Ever? 139
   (*or Will I be Bored on the New Earth?*)
(RIP) Rest in Peace? *or (WIP) Work in Peace?* 149
It's Resurrection, Resurrection, Always Resurrection 159
   (*or No Botox Needed*)
Are Max, Bella, and Jazz in Heaven? 169
May We Sing for Joy to the End of Our Lives (*or In The Wait*) 181
End Notes 189
About the Author 199

The Preparation

We talk about Heaven being so far away. It is within speaking distance to those who belong there. Heaven is a prepared place for a prepared people.

Dwight L. Moody

1

Introduction

For this is how God loved the world: He gave his one and only Son, so that everyone who believes in him will not perish but have eternal life. (John 3:16)

Sunlight streams through the stained-glass windows of the old Presbyterian church. Each window is a tribute to a long-deceased relative of my husband's family—the Fletchers, the McCrarys, the Witherspoons—all just names on a window. I don't know any of them. They all lived and died years ago. As I sit squeezed between two people on the pew, we wait for the service to begin. It's usually a thirty-minute wait because everyone knows you must arrive early to find a seat. The church only holds around one hundred people. We have all lost a dear friend. The packed church is a tribute to her life. It's quiet except for the whispers of the people around me. There's no music yet because the organist hasn't arrived. The ushers walk back and forth, asking people to please scoot in to make room for others.

It always makes me smile when I sit at a funeral, staring at the back of a person's head in front of me and waiting for the service to begin. One of my good friends once told me to let her know if her hair was mussed up in the back. I always give the back of my head a look-see before I leave for the church. Thinking of that, I can't help it. I pat the back of my head.

I finger the bulletin in my hand, turning it over to read the scripture on the front page.

> That is what the Scriptures mean when they say,
> "No eye has seen, no ear has heard,
> and no mind has imagined what God has prepared for
> those who love him. (1 Corinthians 2:9)

I consider this scripture. Later I looked it up in *The Message Bible*: "No one's ever seen or heard anything like this, never so much as imagined anything quite like it—what God has arranged for those who love him."

I have so many questions. We don't think about or hear about Heaven until we go to a friend or family member's funeral. Sitting and waiting for a service to begin gives me time to think.

I first thought about Heaven when my daddy was diagnosed with terminal lung cancer. I was a young mom with three kids. Other than a grandparent, no one close to me had ever died. I will never forget that day. I was sitting in my room at my parents' house as I tried to accept that my daddy was dying. He was the kindest and sweetest man. I don't ever remember him even raising his voice to me. How could I lose him? As I sat in my room, I suddenly felt a joy well up inside of me. How can that be? How could I feel joy? It was as if God gave me a glimpse of Heaven and what awaited my daddy.

Smiling at the thought of my daddy in Heaven, I open the bulletin and read through my friend's obituary—so few words to describe the life of this remarkable woman. She loved Jesus so much. You could see the Holy Spirit all over her. Jesus in her

Introduction

drew all kinds of people. I was sad for her family but happy that she was with her Lord. There is no doubt in my mind that I will see her again.

The organist walks through the door and sits down. She quietly pushes the buttons on the old organ, positions her feet on the pedals, looks out on the crowd, and begins playing beautiful old hymns.

When peace like a river attendeth my way,
when sorrows like sea billows roll;
whatever my lot, thou hast taught me to say,
It is well, it is well with my soul.[1]

And then:

Abide with me, fast falls the eventide;
the darkness deepens; Lord, with me, abide.
When other helpers fail and comforts flee,
Help of the helpless, O abide with me.[2]

Finally:

There's a land that is fairer than day,
And by faith we can see it afar;
For the Father waits over the way
To prepare us a dwelling place there.[3]

These are beautiful hymns written over a hundred years ago by people like us who have tried to reconcile and understand that Heaven awaits and death is not the end. As the sweet music plays, the crowd grows even quieter.

So many questions fill my head. Where is my friend now? Jesus promised the thief on the cross that "today you will be with me in paradise." But where is paradise? What is it like? Will she see her husband there? What does my friend look like now? Has she seen Jesus? I can hear her beautiful southern accent asking him question after question.

As I smile, thinking of this, the preacher walks through the door and gestures for us to stand. It's time to begin.

We all have questions. Is it wrong to think about and yearn for Heaven? Dwight L. Moody, evangelist, and publisher during the Civil War, wrote:

3

"Surely it is not wrong for us to think and talk about Heaven. I like to find out all I can about it. I expect to live there through all eternity. If I were going to dwell in any place in this country, if I were going to make it my home, I would inquire about its climate, about the neighbors I would have – about everything, in fact, that I could learn concerning it. If soon you were going to emigrate, that is the way you would feel. Well, we are all going to emigrate in a very little while. We are going to spend eternity in another world… Is it not natural that we should look and listen and try to find out who is already there and what is the route to take?"[4]

> "Surely it's not wrong for us to think about Heaven."

This book has been churning in me for a while. I am not a scholar or an apologist; I am a teacher. It gives me so much joy and pleasure to take a complex subject, break it down, and explain it in such a way that it is easy to understand. Hopefully, this book will be simple to read and comprehend. It is what it is—my journey to try to understand Heaven.

This year I will be 75 years old. Psalm 90:10 says: "Our days may come to seventy years, or eighty if our strength endures." It hit me not too long ago. I even laughed out loud when I thought about it. I have the lifespan of my dog. Hmm. My beloved dachshund, Max, died two months ago at 14. Only God knows how much longer I have on this earth, but I want to make each day count.

The first thing I researched in writing this book was all the scriptures I could find on eternal life, Heaven, resurrection, and growing old. I pray that God's Word is the bottom line. He is the authority on all things. I believe in the infallibility of God's Word. He is my source.

Another source that inspired me was Randy Alcorn's book, *Heaven*.[5] It helped me to think about Heaven in a new and exciting way. His research was impressive. His description of Heaven gave me substance and a new way of thinking about eternity. Most

Introduction

importantly, he holds the Bible up as his primary authority. His beloved wife, Nanci, died recently from a long battle with cancer. Randy wrote this on Twitter: "All God's children really will live happily ever after. This is not a fairytale; it is the blood-bought promise of Jesus. What a great and kind God He is. As of a few hours ago, Nanci now lives where she sees this firsthand, in the place where Joy truly is the air she breathes."[6]

> *Heaven is not a fairytale.*

Yes, Heaven is really—truly—real. It is not a fairytale. God was delighted to prepare Heaven just for us. But he paid for it through the death and resurrection of Jesus Christ. Paul said this about the resurrection of Jesus:

> But tell me this—since we preach that Christ rose from the dead, why are some of you saying there will be no resurrection of the dead? For if there is no resurrection of the dead, Christ has not been raised either. And if Christ has not been raised, then all our preaching is useless, and your faith is useless. (1 Corinthians 15:12-14)

The early church fathers got it right in the Apostle's Creed.
I believe in God, the Father almighty,
Creator of heaven and earth.
I believe in Jesus Christ, his only Son, our Lord.
He was conceived by the power of the Holy Spirit
and born of the Virgin Mary.
He suffered under Pontius Pilate,
was crucified, died, and was buried.
He descended to the dead.
On the third day, he rose again.
He ascended into heaven,
and is seated at the right hand of the Father.
He will come again to judge the living and the dead.
I believe in the Holy Spirit,
the holy catholic Church*,

the communion of saints,
the forgiveness of sins,
the resurrection of the body,
and the life everlasting. Amen.

*(Meaning *the universal Christian church—all believers in Jesus Christ*

Jesus died on the cross. On the third day, he rose from the dead. He went to Heaven, and he will come again. We will be with him. God said it—I believe it.

This book is divided into three parts. The first part is my thoughts about getting ready for Heaven. This is not morbid or depressing but exciting, like planning a trip. At my age (75), I think about this a lot. First (and most importantly), what about my relationship with Jesus? If I plan to spend eternity with him, I need to start now. Have I accomplished all that God has intended for me to do in my present life? Is my house in order? Will I leave a mess for my kids to clean up after I'm gone? Am I honestly prepared to face the end of my life?

The second part of the book is the Journey to Heaven. How do you get there? What keeps us out of Heaven? How important are friends and family toward the end?

The third part of the book is all about Home—Heaven. I have countless questions. It has been a joy to dig deep into the scriptures and learn from the Holy Spirit as he revealed the delights of eternity and Heaven. Revelation 1:3 says: "God blesses the one who reads the words of this prophecy to the church, and he blesses all who listen to its message and obey what it says, for the time is near." I have been blessed and delighted these last few months as I've taken this journey to Heaven with him. I pray that the reader might catch the joy also.

Soli Deo Gloria

1

Before We Begin to Talk About Heaven

It was the early 1970s. A beautiful lady, Ruth Finley, invited a small group of people to gather in her home and shared with them the experience of the Holy Spirit from the book of Acts. A worldwide movement of the Holy Spirit, the first since the early 1900s, spread across the globe during this time. The group that Ruth brought together consisted of Presbyterians, Methodists, Baptists, and others. Most had never heard of anything like the Baptism of the Holy Spirit, the gifts of the Spirit, or praying in tongues. Lives turned upside down. The "prayer" group began to meet every Thursday night at a couple's house right off Interstate 40.

One night during praise and worship, someone heard a knock at the door. A man and woman stood there with huge smiles on their faces. The host invited them into the house. Their names were Cecil and Joan Pumphrey. They had been driving down Interstate 40 when God told them to get off at the Lonoke exit, and he would tell them where to go from there. He directed them down the road to a house on the right side of the street. Several cars were around it, so they figured that was the house! The group learned Cecil was a minister at Melody Land Church in Anaheim, California. He loved home and foreign mission work and preached in many foreign lands. One of his significant accomplishments was smuggling over 10,000 Bibles into China.

Cecil and Joan often came to the prayer group. He was a remarkable man of God. The one thing that I remember him saying—the one thing that changed my life at the time, and the one thing that inspired me to write this book was what he often said, "I want to walk so close to Jesus here on earth that when I go to Heaven, I will keep right on walking."

Heaven truly begins here on earth. God created us to have a relationship with him. It's as simple as that. Many books end with how to make Jesus the Lord of your life. I want to begin this book with that life-changing act of grace. There's a difference between believing *that* Jesus is a man who lived 2,000 years ago and believing *in* him—having a relationship with him. Before he believed, Thomas had to see the nail scars on Jesus' hand. But Jesus had words for us:

> "Because you have seen me, you have believed; blessed are those who have not seen and yet have believed." Jesus performed many other signs in the presence of his disciples, which are not recorded in this book. But these are written that you may believe that Jesus is the Messiah, the Son of God, and that by believing you may have life in his name. (John 20:29-31, NIV)

That's us! Jesus said we are blessed because we have believed even though we have not seen him.

To have a relationship with someone, you must spend time with them. How do you spend time with the Creator of the Universe? Does he even have time for us? God is omniscient. How is that possible? I think it is a little easier for us to understand this characteristic of God in the twenty-first century than ever before. Computers today keep track of our every move. We can take our

Before We Begin to Talk About Heaven

phone out of our pocket and call someone in France. How far technology has come even in the last twenty years. However, I think God smiles at our trifling attempts at technology. He has engineered the vastness of the universe, the stars, and the galaxies, and then turns around and creates the tiny hummingbird that seemingly defies the gravity he set in place. This God, beyond our imagination or even our comprehension, wants to spend time with you.

> To have a relationship with someone, you must spend time with them.

> Come close to God, and God will come close to you. (James 4:8)

> Don't worry about anything; instead, pray about everything. Tell God what you need and thank him for all he has done. Then you will experience God's peace, which exceeds anything we can understand. His peace will guard your hearts and minds as you live in Christ Jesus. (Philippians 4:6, 7)

What do you do when you spend time with God? It's simple. You know how comfortable you are with your spouse or a good friend when you don't need to say anything. It's the same with God. Some mornings when I wake up and sit in my "prayer" chair, I say, "Lord, I'm here. Thank you for sitting with me this morning." I sit quietly and drink my coffee, enjoying his presence, not saying anything. Other times, I wake up with an urgency to get to God. Perhaps I am troubled or woke up with someone on my mind who needs special prayer. Sometimes I worry about something and say, "I'll talk to God about it tomorrow morning." That lets me put the thought on a shelf without worrying about it.

As I picture Jesus sitting by me on the couch, I look toward him and say, "Lord, thank you. Thank you for all you've done for me—for all you have given me." It's essential to let him know.

Praise God, who did not ignore my prayer or withdraw his

unfailing love from me. (Psalm 66:20)

I praise God for what he has promised; yes, I praise the Lord for what he has promised. (Psalm 56:10)

If you don't know how to praise God, the Psalms are full of scripture like the above that can give voice to your praise. When in doubt, pray the scriptures.

God speaks to us through his Word. To believe, understand, and have a relationship with him, we must read the words he has written to us. We hear this all the time. The Bible is the *Word of God*. It is God himself speaking to us. If we don't read it, we don't hear him. It's as simple as that. There are many different translations these days. There's no need to purchase several different ones as we used to because we can open our phones and have them at our fingertips. If you don't understand one translation, finding a different one is perfectly okay. Don't feel less spiritual if you read from a translation like *The Living Bible*[1] or *The Message Bible*.[2] A new Bible that I have enjoyed lately is the *NLT Immerse Bible: The Reading Bible: Messiah*.[3] The *Immerse Bible* has no chapter titles, verse numbers, or footnotes. Sometimes it's good to read God's Word without distractions—God speaking to you without commentary from other voices.

There are many ways to read God's Word. Sometimes I ask, "Lord, what do you have to say to me today?" Then I randomly open the Bible and begin to read. It's amazing how God speaks to me on that page. Sometimes when I ask for a "word" for someone I am praying for, God will put that word in my mind. At the top of the *YouVersion* Bible app[4] is a search window where I can type in a word. Scriptures pop up with that word in italics. So often, those scriptures are just what that person needs to hear. It's also important to read everything in context. Reading entire books of the Bible gives you a better understanding of what God is saying. Daily pouring over God's Word keeps you in a relationship with him. The only way to know God's Will is to read God's Word.

Bible study is another excellent way to dig into God's Word.

Before We Begin to Talk About Heaven

There are hundreds of studies. Many are accessible online. Bible study focuses on a theme or a book of the Bible. Connecting with other Christians in Bible study brings you together with the Body of Christ.

What if you don't know Jesus? Would you take an all-expenses paid vacation to the most beautiful place on Earth if someone offered it to you? Would you accept if they said that your family could accompany you and that this delightful vacation would never end? Would you pack today if they guaranteed you would never be sick on this vacation, never worry, and experience the sweetest peace you have ever had? God doesn't promise that we will experience this vacation on Earth. Let's face it. Even with Jesus, life on Earth can be difficult, but God promises never to leave or forsake us until we depart this Earth to enjoy Heaven. That's what we get when we accept Jesus as our Savior, the Lord of our life, and our tour guide to Heaven. It's simple. You don't have to be super spiritual or even "good." God loves you and wants a relationship with you.

> God promises never to leave or forsake us until we depart this Earth to enjoy Heaven.

If we choose to live apart from him. If we decide to go our way and do our own thing. God calls this sin.

> "For the wages of sin is death, but the free gift of God is eternal life through Christ Jesus our Lord.
> (Romans 6:23)
>
> For this is how God loved the world: He gave his one and only Son so that everyone who believes in him will not perish but have eternal life. (John 3:16)

God loved us and wanted to restore our relationship so much that he sent Jesus to die on the cross for us.

> "Christ suffered for our sins once for all time. He never sinned,

but he died for sinners to bring them safely home to God. He suffered physical death, but he was raised to life in the Spirit. (1 Peter 3:18)

So, how do you respond? What happens now?

If you openly declare that Jesus is Lord and believe in your heart that God raised him from the dead, you will be saved. For it is by believing in your heart that you are made right with God, and it is by openly declaring your faith that you are saved. As the Scriptures tell us, "Anyone who trusts in him will never be disgraced." Jew and Gentile are the same in this respect. They have the same Lord, who gives generously to all who call on him. For "Everyone who calls on the name of the Lord will be saved." (Romans 10:9-13)

Going to church does not save you. Having Christian parents or grandparents does not save you. Neither does teaching a Bible study, tithing, supporting a missionary, or other "good Christian deeds." Jesus is the only one who can do that because he wants a relationship with you. "Anyone who trusts in him will never be disgraced" (Romans 10:11). You can't trust someone you don't know.

> Look! I stand at the door and knock. If you hear my voice and open the door, I will come in, and we will share a meal together as friends. (Revelation 3:20)

There's a famous painting by Warner Sallman[5] of Jesus standing at a wooden door surrounded by beautiful ivy. He has his hand up as if he is getting ready to knock. When I was four, I remember a neighborhood lady inviting several neighbor children into her home. I don't remember her name or if my family even knew her. She showed us the picture of Jesus at the door and asked if we wanted to invite Jesus into our hearts. I will never forget that. My family did not go to church very much then, so she

Before We Begin to Talk About Heaven

was the first person to introduce me to Jesus. As a four-year-old, I didn't understand the Jesus in my heart part, but I know now, 71 years later, that God placed his hand on my head, and that's when I became his friend.

I look forward to sharing a meal with Jesus and that neighborhood lady when I reach Heaven.

Heaven! That's what this book is all about. I can't wait to share everything I've learned about eternity. But first, we must get to the *getting old* part.

> Even to your old age and gray hairs
> I am he; I am he who will sustain you.
> I have made you, and I will carry you.
> I will sustain you, and I will rescue you. (Isaiah 46:4, NIV)

Light-seeds

Light is sown for the righteous, and joy on the upright in heart. Psalm 97:11

What kind of relationship do you have with God?

How do you spend time with Jesus?

"Blessed are those who have not seen and believe" (John 20: 29). That's you! What is God saying to you in this scripture?

"To have a relationship with someone, you must spend time with them." How has God spoken to you—specifically—through his Word?

Do you honestly believe that God wants a relationship with you?

2

Getting Old is Heck *(or Not)*

My mother lived to be 84 years old. As she got older and began to have health problems, she would laugh and tell me, "Getting old is heck." That didn't stop her, however, from enjoying her life. People always thought that she looked young for her age because she acted young. She drove her bridge club friends to Little Rock the morning before she died. That night she was in Heaven. Sad for me, but happy for her; she died on the evening of my 55th birthday. My granddaughter had just been born, and I was in Washington, DC, with my daughter. It isn't easy to lose someone without getting to say goodbye. But then, it's also difficult watching someone waste away and suffer before they pass on. There's no easy way to die, but truth be told, we don't have a choice. As I boarded the plane to fly back to Arkansas, I thanked God that my mother didn't suffer and that she enjoyed her life of 83 years.

The quote, "Old age ain't no place for sissies," has been attributed to the screen star, Bette Davis. I understand what she was saying. Yes, there are aches, pains, illnesses, and all the physical problems that come with old age, but as aging Christians, we can experience wisdom, joy, and satisfaction from a well-lived life. A metamorphosis is happening in me as I grow older year by year. Dallas Willard expressed my very thoughts:

> "Aging, accordingly, will become a process not of losing, but of gaining. As our physical body fades out, our glory body approaches and our spiritual substance grows richer and deeper. As we age, we should become obviously more glorious."[1]

I love that. To become "more glorious" because of the One who lives in me is a good thing.

The person I see in the mirror or a photograph can't be me because I still feel thirty years old. It's interesting to think that even though my body is growing old, my spirit only gets younger. The reason is that my spirit and soul are eternal. God created me in his image. God is eternal, and so am I. Mark Twain once quipped, "Life would be infinitely happier if we could only be born at the age of 80 and gradually approach 18."[2] Well, Mark, if you had read your Bible, you would have learned that is exactly what God says happens to us. He also promises that there will come a time when he gives us a resurrected body that eventually joins eternally with our young spirit and soul.

> For you have been born again, but not to a life that will quickly end. Your new life will last forever because it comes from the eternal, living word of God.
>
> As the Scriptures say, "People are like grass; their beauty is like a flower in the field. The grass withers and the flower fades. But the word of the Lord remains forever." And that word is the Good News that was preached to you. (1 Peter 1:23-25)

People have always searched for ways to stay young or live forever. Legend has it that Ponce de León searched for the fountain of youth. Isaac Newton dabbled in alchemy, a medieval science that searched for a way to change base metals into gold to cure diseases and prolong life. Diane de Poitiers, reputedly the most beautiful woman in 16th-century France, drank gold to preserve her good looks. Heinrich Himmler, the insidious architect of the Holocaust in Nazi Germany, embarked on a failed mission to find the Holy Grail in 1940, visiting an abbey perched within the Montserrat mountain range in Catalonia. He believed the Holy Grail would give him superhuman powers and eternal life (think Indiana Jones). In today's world, wealthy billionaires like Richard Bezos (Amazon), Larry Ellison (Oracle), Peter Thiel (PayPal), and the Saudi royal family are investing millions into longevity research.

> You saw me before I was born. Every day of my life was recorded in your book. Every moment was laid out before a single day had passed. (Psalm 139:16)

> No one can control the wind or lock it in a box.
> No one has any say-so regarding the day of death.
> (Ecclesiastes 8:8, Message)

Even biologists will tell you that every cell in our body has mortality programmed within it. We are all born to die. When Adam sinned, he experienced spiritual death—separation from God. He later experienced physical death. Medicine has made incredible progress in our lifetime, but mortality is still 100 percent.

Do you remember the song, *Fame,* by Irene Cara?[3]

"I'm gonna live forever
I'm gonna learn how to fly (High)
I feel it coming together
People will see me and cry
I'm gonna make it to Heaven
Light up the sky like a flame
I'm gonna live forever
Baby, remember my name."

Yes, we all want to live forever—we want to be remembered, and if we're honest, we want to stay young.

I don't recall my mother, mother-in-law, grandmothers, or

aunts taking extreme measures to look young. They aged with grace and beauty beyond Botox or plastic surgery. (Thinking back, my Aunt Louise *did* continue to color her hair until her 90's.) These ladies embraced their aging bodies and faces by always dressing nicely, getting their hair "done" weekly, and having youthful smiles.

The Bible has so much to say about aging and promises that God will always be with us even in our old age:

> Is not wisdom found among the aged?
> Does not long life bring understanding? (Job 12:12, NIV)

We will continue to bear fruit, be useful, and thrive as we age:

> The righteous will flourish like a palm tree, they will grow like a cedar of Lebanon; planted in the house of the Lord, they will flourish in the courts of our God. *They will still bear fruit in old age,* they will stay fresh and green, proclaiming, "The Lord is upright; he is my Rock, and there is no wickedness in him." (Psalm 92:12-15, NIV)

The important thing is to live each day God gives to us in a way that glorifies him. In Billy Graham's book, *Nearing Home: Thoughts on Life, Faith, and Finishing Well,* he writes: "When granted many years of life, growing old in age is natural, but growing old with grace is a choice. Growing older with grace is possible for all who will set their hearts and minds on the Giver of grace, the Lord Jesus Christ."[4] Dr. Graham firmly believed God had a reason for keeping us here on earth. If he didn't, he would have already taken us to Heaven.

> "Growing old with grace is a choice."
> Billy Graham

So how do we live out the rest of our lives with grace, no matter how long or short it might be? God created us to be born, live our lives, and grow old with him. He has a purpose for us. He is not going to ditch us. Here's a conversation that I have had with God:

Getting Old is Heck *(or Not)*

Me: "But Lord, I don't have the energy I used to have. I can't do what I used to do. I'm not able to . . ."

God: "Don't have? Can't do it? Not able to? Part of that is true. Your body *is* gradually wasting away, but here's the deal. I am revitalizing your days. Your troubles will not last long in the scheme of things. I choose to keep you around a little longer because I will use you in a way that outweighs any problems you might have right now. So, fix your eyes on glory! Fix your eyes on me! You can't even imagine what I have planned for you." (2 Corinthians 4:16-18, CV, Cindy's Version)

In a recent article in *Christianity Today* entitled *The Church Is Losing Its Greyheads* (2022), Adam McCinnis quoted research from the Barna Institute which stated that some of the most significant declines in church attendance over the past three decades have been among adults 55 and older.[5] In a study in 2011, Bama Research said that Boomers (those born between 1946 and 1964) are the most likely to be unchurched.[6] What's up with that? After Covid, many older adults never came back into a church building. Sitting on the couch and watching church on TV is so easy. I can identify with that! My husband and I were two couch sitters during Covid. It was nice not to have to get dressed or leave the house. But then the Holy Spirit began to nudge.

> *"It's not about us, is it, Lord?"*
> *"Nope"*

Let us think of ways to motivate one another to acts of love and good works. And let us not neglect our meeting together, as some people do, but encourage one another, especially now that the day of his return is drawing near. (Hebrews 10:24, 25)

Boomers have approached retirement differently than their grandparents. Many are still working way up into their 70s.

They're not really into potlucks, teas, or bus trips. Some blame the church for not being relevant or not meeting their needs, but I don't think that's the problem. The problem is with us. God doesn't want other people to meet our spiritual needs as we walk through the rest of our days. That can only lead to disappointment and depression as aging becomes more difficult.

God created us to work for him and to have a relationship with him. How do we do that effectively? Here's the deal, we don't serve to say we're "on a committee," but we serve after we *pray for direction* and *truly listen to his voice*. That way, we continue to make a difference in his kingdom.

How we serve now may not be how we helped when we were younger, but that is okay. The Body of Christ consists of many parts. We may have been his feet in the past, but now we're his arms or voice. "Even when I am old and gray, do not forsake me, my God, till I declare your power to the next generation, your mighty acts to all who are to come" (Psalm 71:18, NIV). Declare his power to the next generation—your grandchildren, nieces, nephews, or family friends. That might be your assignment until he takes you home. God can even use someone in a nursing home by praying for others and blessing those around them. It's all a matter of believing you are where he wants you to be and doing what he wants you to do.

> Even in old age, they will still produce fruit;
> they will remain vital and green. (Psalm 92:14)

So many people in the Bible have modeled old age for us. God kept some of these people around a lot longer than he's keeping us these days.

God told Adam in Genesis 1:28 to "Be fruitful and increase in number; fill the earth and subdue it" (NIV). Adam lived to be 930 years old. "After Seth was born, Adam lived 800 years and had other sons and daughters" (Genesis 5:4, NIV). There are ten men listed in Genesis 5, from Adam to Noah. All of them lived to be around 900 years old! You can imagine how many children

Getting Old is Heck *(or Not)*

they had. After the flood, people gradually began to have shorter life spans. Some say it was because they started eating meat for the first time. "Everything that lives and moves about will be food for you. Just as I gave you the green plants; I now give you everything" (Genesis 9:3, NIV). Some say it was due to the gene pool (family marrying family?) over the centuries. Some think God altered the earth's atmosphere after the flood.

Gradually, over the centuries, lifespans became shorter and shorter. God used Adam, Enoch, and Noah even more so as they aged. We know that "Enoch lived 365 years, walking in close fellowship with God. Then one day he disappeared because God took him" (Genesis 5:23, 24). God just enjoyed his company! Noah didn't even begin his ark until he was in his 500s.

Abraham didn't meet God until he was 75 years old. He lived for another 100 years and accomplished so much in those years. Abraham left his gods, homeland, his comfortable life and moved to a strange land. He had no Bible, no priest or preacher to guide him. God spoke to him, and he obeyed. That's faith. Imagine the twinkle in God's eye when he told Abraham and Sarah that they would be parents at their age!

Joseph, Moses, Miriam, Aaron, and Joshua lived over one hundred years. Think of the aches and pains—arthritis—they endured. The last Old Testament hero to live well past a century was King Jehoiada. He led the Kingdom of Judah back to the Lord. When he died, he received one of its most significant honors. "He was buried with the kings in the City of David, because of the good he had done in Israel for God and his temple" (2 Chronicles 24:16, NIV).

We know that David died at around 71 years old. He was thirty then he became king and reigned for 40 years. "He died at a ripe old age, having enjoyed long life, wealth, and honor" (1 Chronicles 29:28). That's interesting that it says that he died at a ripe old age. We all want to be "ripe"' when we die.

My five favorite New Testament senior saints were Elisabeth, Zachariah, Anna, Simeon, and John. Even in their old age, God blessed Elisabeth and Zachariah with a baby boy—a child who grew up to be the forerunner to Jesus. Simeon waited his entire life to hold the king of the universe in his arms: "Sovereign Lord, now let your servant die in peace, as you have promised. I have seen your salvation, which you have prepared for all people. He is a light to reveal God to the nations, and he is the glory of your people Israel" (Luke 2:29-32)! Anna was an eighty-five-year-old widow who prayed in the temple day and night. God gave her the privilege of prophesying over baby Jesus. I can't even imagine. And finally, John. John was the only disciple to live to a ripe old age. He wrote the final book of the Bible—Revelation.

God purposely used these people to be a model for us as we age. There is no retirement from the Kingdom of God. He has allowed us to live these many years so that he can use our experiences and wisdom to further his kingdom. My relationship with my adult children now differs from when they were young. Just as we enjoy our children, God enjoys being with us, regardless of our age.

> There is no retirement from the Kingdom of God.

Yes, old age can be difficult, painful, uncomfortable, and heck, but God reminds us that it's worth it. There's a promise waiting for us on the other side.

> Our citizenship is in Heaven. And we eagerly await a Savior from there, the Lord Jesus Christ, who, by the power that enables him to bring everything under his control, will transform our lowly bodies so that they will be like his glorious body. (Philippians 3:20, 21, NIV)

Getting Old is Heck *(or Not)*

Light-seeds

As our physical body fades out, our glory body approaches, and our spiritual substance grows richer and deeper. As we age, we become obviously *more glorious*. How 'bout that!

How is your spiritual substance growing richer?

Are we caught up in preserving our youth rather than our spirit?

How does the Bible teach us about aging as compared to the world?

Do you know someone who is growing old with grace?

If you truly believe God created you to work for him and have a relationship with him, how do you do this effectively, even in old age?

Who is your Old Testament or New Testament model for growing old with grace?

There is no retirement from the Kingdom of God. What does that mean to you?

Walk Me Into Heaven

3

The Courage to Get to the End

Punching in the numbers, I slip through the nursing home's front door, giving a quick smile to the young man in a wheelchair stationed by the door. He's always there when I come in, moved there, perhaps, where he can see the comings and goings of the visitors. He doesn't smile but stares straight ahead. Walking past him, I ease down the hall past the woman wheeling herself one foot at a time in her wheelchair. Intent on her journey, she ignores me. Quietly I knock on the first door on the right. Peeking in, I see that Mrs. Ruby is sleeping. Her roommate smiles and says, "Now, go right ahead and wake her, honey; she won't want to miss your visit." Hesitantly, I call her name, "Mrs. Ruby.... Mrs. Ruby, it's me, Cindy."

Mrs. Ruby stirred and turned toward me, groggy and incoherent for a moment until recognition set in, and then she gave me a huge smile. Every time I see her, she blesses me with that beautiful smile, smiling with her entire face, nose wrinkling, and bright eyes sparkling with fun, intelligence, and pure love. As I reached to hug her, Mrs. Ruby trembled joyfully and tried to sit up, her thin shoulders shaking. She began talking to me as I eased her back on her bed. I could make out only some of her words because, after several mini-strokes, Mrs. Ruby's speech was difficult to understand. But that doesn't stop her! I tell her about my children and grandchildren, and she tells me about her daughter and her beloved grandson, Stan. Listening intently, I get the gist of what she is trying to say to me. Love is our language. We understand each other perfectly.

Mrs. Ruby is teaching me about grace and courage—and dignity. She has fallen, broken bones, and faced surgery without complaint. But Mrs. Ruby serenely embraces each day, knowing her Lord always cares for her. Every time I am with her, I feel the presence of the Lord; yes, even God-bumps in her tiny nursing home room.

Over the years, Mrs. Ruby has prayed for many people, sent out church bulletins to those absent because of sickness or vacations, and been a quiet presence in the church. She tells me about people she is still praying for from her nursing home bed. God will continue to use Mrs. Ruby until the day He takes her home to be with Him.

We pray together before I leave, her beautiful eyes glistening with tears of love for her Lord and me. Reluctantly, she lets go of my hand. It's always so difficult to leave her. I tell her roommate goodbye and ask her to take care of Mrs. Ruby. Her roommate smiles fondly at her. "Honey, I can't hear, and she can't talk, but Lord, we get along just great!"

I am always humbled when I punch those numbers back in and walk out the front door of that nursing home. Taking in the beautiful sunset as I drive home, I pray that someday I might have the courage and dignity Mrs. Ruby is teaching me. Proverbs 31:25 says, "She is clothed with strength and dignity, and she laughs without fear of the future."

"Yet I am always with you;
You hold me by my right hand.
You guide me with your counsel
And afterward, you will take me into glory.

> Whom have I in Heaven but you?
> And earth has nothing I desire besides you.
> My flesh and my heart may fail,
> But God is the strength of my heart
> And my portion forever. (Psalm 73:23-26, NIV)

We might all prefer to choose how we die. But the reality is—we can't. We can't choose the day, the hour, or the way.

> In their hearts, humans plan their course, but the Lord establishes their steps. (Proverbs 16:9, NIV)

> I can make the perfect plan, but God has the last say. (Proverbs 16:9, Cindy's Version)

> As no one has power over the wind to contain it, so no one has power over the time of their death. (Ecclesiastics 8:8, NIV)

Peace can only come when I give God absolute, categorical, and complete control of each day of my life. I can't conjure up enough adjectives to state this essential fact. We can worry and fret about the future, but that won't add one more day; it will just make us miserable. We must trust God and fully live each day he gives us. Paul said, "I eagerly expect and hope that I will in no way be ashamed but will have sufficient courage so that now as always Christ will be exalted in my body, whether by life or by death. For to me, to live is Christ, and to die is gain" (Philippians 1:20,21, NIV).

> *Peace can only come when I give God complete control of each day of my life.*

My grandmother was ill for the last few years of her life. One day she sat on the couch, took a deep breath, and entered Heaven. Another precious lady, Ms. Bessie Jane, died the same way. Her daughter had flown in to have a nice long visit with her mother. She hadn't been home in a while. They were sitting together in

Walk Me Into Heaven

her living room reading the paper, and Ms. Bessie Jane took her last breath and was in Heaven.

On the other hand, my daddy died of lung cancer—an excruciating and difficult way to die. Through it, however, we were able to be with him, say our goodbyes, and walk with him on that last journey. We walked the same journey with my mother-in-law. Watching her suffer from cancer was heartbreaking, but God never left her or us during her illness. This precious lady spent her whole life serving and caring for her family. During her illness, we were finally able to serve and take care of her. As is often the case, she walked into Heaven the morning after her oldest granddaughter came home to say goodbye.

Family is so important during these times. There is a sweetness and closeness as families surround the death of a loved one. During the last few days of my brother's life, his children, grandchildren, wife, and ex-wife gathered in his hospital room, reminiscing, laughing, crying, and praying with him. Even though my brother was in a coma, we spoke to him, held his hand, and told him how much we loved him. My brother loved his family. I believe he heard and felt all of it.

It is heartbreaking to watch a family member or friend slowly fade away with dementia or Alzheimer's. My family walked that difficult journey with my husband's father. After making the agonizing decision to place him in a nursing home, my mother-in-law sat with him from early morning to evening every day. She lovingly made sure that the nursing home staff met all his needs.

I have a beautiful and sweet friend who is now housebound, spending her days napping and watching TV in the loving care of her daughter and caregivers. This woman was a whirlwind. She was an educator who loved to be with people and children. Through her seventies and early eighties, she tutored children, checked in on friends, baked her delicious pound cake, worked at the church, and ensured everyone remembered her beloved Carver School. Most importantly, she loved Jesus.

This poem by CT Studd (1860-1931) sums up my friend:
"Only one life, yes, only one,

Now let me say, 'Thy will be done.'
And when, at last, I'll hear the call,
I know I'll say 'twas worth it all.
Only one life 'twill soon be past,
Only what's done for Christ will last."[1]

These last couple of years could indeed be called her twilight years. The light in her eyes is dimming, but a presence in her room gives me a sense of peace—God's presence. I have tried to visit her as often as possible. Most days, she still recognizes me. I love walking into her room and seeing her sweet face light up. We talk of the past, the children we have taught, and her childhood. Some days are better than others. Before I leave my friend, I often ask her if I can pray for her. Even if she has not been very responsive during the visit, she will look directly at me and smile. The other day after I prayed, I said, "Mrs. Lillie, God is good, isn't he?" As clear as day, she replied, "All the time."

> God is good–all the time.

How do I know this? How do I know that somewhere within my friend is her eternal spirit—a spirit that is alive and well—waiting to be set free?

In 2014, *World Magazine* posted an update on Elisabeth Elliott. Elisabeth is well known as the wife of Jim Elliott, a missionary martyred in Ecuador in 1956. After his death, she remained in Ecuador, ministering to the people who had killed her husband. Elisabeth married again in 1969, but her husband died of cancer four years later. She married for the final time in 1977 to Lars Gren. During her life, she wrote 28 books.

Tiffany Owens, a reporter for *World Magazine*, traveled to Massachusetts to meet Elisabeth and Lars and shared the encounter:

> Lars Gren led me down a dim hallway to a simple room lit magnificently by floor-to-ceiling windows that looked out over the Atlantic Ocean. A slim, elderly woman dressed in black pants and a floral shirt — her

hair swirled in a bun — sat near the fireplace. "We have company today," Gren said, bending down to touch her hand. His wife, Elisabeth Elliot, nodded but did not reply.

When Elisabeth realized she was losing her memory, she put into practice what she had long preached: "From acceptance comes peace." Her husband said she turned to the Bible for comfort, especially Isaiah 43:2: "When you pass through the waters, I will be with you; and through the rivers, they shall not overwhelm you; when you walk through the fire, you shall not be burned, and the flame shall not consume you."

Since the onset of dementia about a decade ago, the best-selling and widely known Christian author communicates mostly through slight hand gestures and facial expressions. For everything else, there's Lars, her husband of 36 years. He and two caregivers attend to her daily needs.

Gren says Elliot has handled dementia just as she did the deaths of her husbands. "She accepted those things, [knowing] they were no surprise to God," Gren said. "She would rather not have experienced it, but she received it."

Hearing these words, Elisabeth looked up and nodded, her eyes clear and strong. Then she spoke for the first time during the two-hour interview, nodding vigorously: "Yes."[2]

At Elisabeth's funeral, Steve Saint—son of Nate Saint, one of the other missionaries killed alongside Elliot's first husband—honored Elizabeth saying this:

"I think Elizabeth would be happy just being remembered as not much of a woman that God used greatly. To the rest of us mortals, she was an incredibly talented and gifted woman who trusted God in life's greatest calamities, even the loss of her mind to dementia, and who allowed God to use her. He did use her. Tens of thousands of people will mourn her loss. I will certainly be one of them. But isn't it incredibly wonderful that our loss is certainly her gain? She can think and talk once again!"[3]

Yes, just like God used Elisabeth, my sweet friend, Lillie, is still being used by God.

Walk Me Into Heaven

Light-seeds

Do you worry about the future? Are you afraid?

How do you honestly trust God to take care of you to the end—no matter what?

Only one life 'twill soon be past.
Only what's done for Christ will last.
What will people remember about you?

No matter what—as a Christ-follower, God uses our life for his glory. Do you know someone whose life God still uses even though the world has written them off?

"Peace can only come when I give . . . ."
Is it possible to give God complete control of your life?

4

College Hunks Hauling Junk or (You Can't Take it With You)

Several years ago, after recovering from a year-long battle with breast cancer, I decided to get rid of *stuff*. Finally getting my strength back, the first place to tackle had to be "The ATTIC!" Our home has a huge attic that covers the entire length of our house. It was a fun place for the kids to play when they were young, but I kept putting stuff up there. Maybe I would use it. Maybe the kids or grandkids would want it. If my husband saw me hauling something out of the attic, he would ask, "Are you throwing that away? It might be worth a fortune someday." I knew that *someday* my kids would have to face "The ATTIC." I didn't want them to say, "Didn't Mom ever throw anything away?"

I was a woman on a mission. Who would carry it off for me? Where would it go? I didn't want to ask my son to help, and my husband would put things back because of the *Are you throwing that away—it might be worth a fortune* attitude. So, I got online and found a company called *College Hunks Hauling Junk.*®[1] (Yes, that's the name of their company.) I learned their name was an acronym that meant Honest, Uniformed, Nice, Knowledgeable, and Service. So, the *hunk* part was just a hook. That was okay. I needed some muscle to get things done, and these were the guys for the job.

Two young guys arrived in an orange and green bob truck a week later. I was doubtful that all my junk could go inside it, but they seemed to know what they were doing. They followed me up the stairs to the attic and looked around. Taking a determined breath, I started pointing. "Take that—and that. Yep, that goes, too." In a short time, they had loaded the truck with our stuff. They told me that 70% of it would be recycled or donated. I didn't care. I just wanted it gone.

An organized home is one of the greatest gifts we can leave for our children. In an article from *Modern Loss*, a website encouraging candid conversations about grief, Shira Gill suggests five steps to streamline our stuff so "our family won't have to."[2] I have added my responses to her five steps.

> An organized home is one of the greatest gifts we can leave for our children.

1. *Organize your documents.* Several years ago, my husband and I organized all our important papers, like insurance forms, our will, and business documents into two boxes. My son-in-law is a list maker, so I made a list sheet that detailed everything in those boxes. (You're welcome, Robert.)
2. *Document your valuables.* I need to work on this. There are a few paintings and jewelry that I have placed notes on to let my kids know where they came from and how much they are worth.
3. *Minimize your media.* During Covid, I was determined to digitize all my old VHS tapes and put them on a disc for each of my kids. I borrowed an old VHS player and purchased an *Elgato Video Capture*[3] device that connected my computer to the VHS player. It wasn't as difficult as

I thought it would be. It did take *forever,* but, hey, it was during the "lockdown." What else did I have to do? I also sent off our Super 8 movies and had them digitized.

4. *Ditch the duplicates.* Periodically, I purge my coffee cups. (I *really* like to collect those.) If I have two of something, I try to give it away. I also go through my clothes each season, and if I have not worn something in a year and I don't "love it," then I give it away to someone who will. Now, with my husband, that's a different story. He tells me that "maybe" someday he will wear a particular shirt or coat. So, if he's not around, that's a good time to go through his clothes. He never even misses them.

5. *Ruthlessly Edit Your Memorabilia.* I am not very sentimental about my things. When I clean out a closet or go through my stuff, I often say to myself, "Nobody cares. Nobody cares." That's not anything against my kids, but the things that I have held on to probably are not things my kids will want to keep. And that's okay. Several years ago, I was at a friend's house. She proudly showed me an entire wall of lovely China dishes she and her husband had collected over many years. He had even built an exquisite lighted cabinet to display them. She told me that when they built the cabinet, they hoped their kids would someday enjoy the dishes as much as they had. She smiled sadly and said, "But I know they won't. This was our joy, not theirs."

Several years after the Hunks had come, I returned to the attic to finish the job. I sorted through the broken and dusty boxes filled with brittle papers, warped photos, and childhood memories. I carefully pulled out a few things like photos I thought my family might enjoy someday, took pictures of the different things left, and then sent them all to the trash. My attic is now clean except for a few boxes of my kids' stuff (that they probably won't want), important papers that we will keep for five years for tax purposes, and Christmas boxes. Walking up there and seeing an empty attic is a good feeling.

Walk Me Into Heaven

Photographs are another thing in the house that weighed on me every time I tried to pry open a couple of drawers full of photos. Several years ago, I purchased three photo boxes with handles, one for each of my kids. I started pulling photos out of picture albums and out of drawers. I began dividing up the photos among the three boxes. I didn't get caught up in labeling or sorting by the same years. It was more like baby, childhood, teen, and adult photos. Someday, each kid can pick up one photo box and return it to their home.

I have a few boxes of mementos from my mother and mother-in-law. They contain photos, letters sent back and forth to their husbands during WWII, newspaper articles, etc. One day while one of my daughters was home, I asked her to go through them. I wanted to answer her questions about the things in the box. I wish I had asked more questions when my mother and mother-in-law were alive.

> About that time, Hezekiah became deathly ill, and the prophet Isaiah son of Amoz, went to visit him. He gave the king this message: "This is what the Lord says: 'Set your affairs in order, for you are going to die. You will not recover from this illness.'" (Isaiah 38:1)

There's a law firm in Arkansas whose motto is "If you have a dollar and two relatives, you need to do some estate planning."[4] It's heartbreaking to hear families arguing over money, jewelry, or possessions after a family member has died. It was once said, "I have never seen a hearse hauling a U-Haul." We can't take it with us, so we need to have a plan to distribute it in our will. According to the 2021 Gallup Poll, more than half (55%) of Americans die yearly without a legal will or trust.[5] As Christians who look forward to Heaven, we should not hesitate to plan for our death. It is irresponsible from a stewardship perspective not to complete an estate plan. Death and illness are times filled with emotion; we don't want to add to the stress on our family by leaving our finances in disorder. Brett Widness explains it well:

"If you die without a valid will, you'll become *intestate*. That means your estate will be settled based on the laws of your state that outline who inherits what. *Probate* is the legal process of transferring a deceased person's property to the rightful heirs.

Since no executor is named, a judge appoints an administrator to serve in that capacity. An administrator will also be named if a will is deemed invalid. All wills must meet specific standards, such as being witnessed, to be legally valid. Again, requirements vary from state to state.

An administrator will most likely be a stranger to you and your family, and he or she will be bound by the letter of your state's probate laws. As such, an administrator may make decisions that wouldn't necessarily agree with your wishes or those of your heirs."[6]

But those who won't care for their relatives, especially those in their own household, have denied the true faith. Such people are worse than unbelievers. (1 Timothy 5:8)

You don't have to hire a lawyer to write your will. If it meets your state's legal requirements, you're good to go, whether a lawyer wrote it or you wrote it on the back of a napkin. (Which is probably not recommended.) If you write it yourself (and there are many kits online), find someone, not a beneficiary, to witness your signature. Some states require that you have your will notarized. That sounds like a good idea.

"Abraham lived for 175 years, and he died at a ripe old age, having lived a long and satisfying life. He breathed his last and joined his ancestors in death. His sons Isaac and Ishmael buried him in the cave of Machpelah, near Mamre, in the field of Ephron son of Zohar the Hittite. This was the field Abraham had purchased from the Hittites and where he had buried his wife, Sarah." (Genesis 25:7-10)

Abraham planned ahead. He had already purchased the burial cave for his precious wife, Sarah. His sons knew to bury him beside her. There was no question in their mind. Knowing our wishes ahead of time is helpful to our family. Notice that when Abraham dies, the two stepbrothers, Isaac and Ishmael, join to bury their father. These two "boys" would now be 75 and 89, respectively. It's interesting to note that the Bible mentioned the younger son first. According to Naomi Kalish from the Jewish Theological Seminary, "The Midrash interprets this to mean that Ishmael engaged in a process of *teshuvah*, repentance. One may read the word teshuvah as "repentance" or simply as "return." Ishmael returned—to his estranged brother. For reasons we do not know, he gestured for his brother to lead the way."[7] Abraham must have smiled in Heaven, knowing that his two boys stood side by side in that burial cave. Heaven rejoices when families reconcile. Unfortunately, that is not always the case.

> Heaven rejoices when families reconcile.

The last thing that you need to "put your house in order" is to have an Advance Medical Directive. An article entitled *Discussing Your Medical Wishes: A Patient's Guide* by Carrie Earl says: "The Living Will Declaration is discouraged, as it is a signed statement that attempts to predict your preferences in often complex future medical situations you cannot foresee. The statement offers a narrow list of options that may be used to prohibit treatment you may want in a certain circumstance — even for a short period of time." (This puts the power in the hands of a physician who may or may not be on the same page as you are).

Earl says that a "Durable Power of Attorney for Health Care is encouraged as it allows you to name a trusted family member or friend to make medical decisions for you if you're unable to do so."[8] When a power of attorney is "durable," your agent's authority to act on your behalf continues even if you become incapacitated. A nondurable power of attorney expires and is no longer valid if you become incapacitated. Because of this, medical powers of attorney are written to be durable—they don't come into effect unless you become debilitated. Durable POAs are often used to prepare for a situation when important decisions need to be made, but you can't make them yourself. The key is to discuss your end-of-life wishes with your family and the person you designated as your Durable Medical Power of Attorney.

I came across an Advanced Directive form called *Five Wishes*.[9] This form lets your family and doctor know the following:
- Whom do you want to make health care decisions for you when you can't make them?
- The kind of medical treatment you want or don't want.
- How comfortable do you want to be?
- How do you want people to treat you?
- What do you want your loved ones to know?

This form would be an excellent place to discuss your end-of-life wishes with your family.

My husband and I have a Living Will, but we also have a Durable Power of Attorney. We are each other's DPOA until the day one of us walks into Heaven. We will appoint our three children to be our DPOA at that time. We trust these three amazing adults to care for us and respect our wishes.

Whew! Now that we've covered all that, let's talk about Heaven!

Light-seeds

Cleaning out, sorting, organizing, and throwing away: It can make a person want to grab a book or take a nice long nap. Where is *one* place you can begin?

How can you preserve your history without overwhelming your family?

Do you have a Will? A Living Will? A Power of Attorney?

How are "those who don't care for their relatives worse than unbelievers?" 1 Timothy 5:8

Have you been clear—precise—exact in letting your family know your end-of-life wishes?

The Journey

He has shown you O mortal, what is good.
And what does the Lord require of you?
To act justly and to love mercy
and to walk humbly with your God.

Micah 6:8

5

Traveling Toward Heaven

> From now on every road you travel
> Will take you to God.
> Follow the Covenant signs;
> Read the charted directions.
> (Psalm 25:10, Message)

Several years ago, I flew from Arkansas to Massachusetts to attend a "silent retreat" at the St. Joseph Retreat Center in Cohasset, MA. The eight days were devoted to silence, prayer, and being with God. It was so easy and so peaceful. At the end of my week, my husband, Preston (a pilot), suggested I rent a car, drive from Cohasset to New York, and catch a flight home to Arkansas with him. I was game. In the rental was a simple GPS that would help me find Preston. He told me I would be fine, *but don't go over the bridge*, and don't end up in New York City! (This was the first time I had ever traveled with a GPS. It wasn't even on my phone or programmed in the vehicle, but a device propped on the dashboard.) Remember those?

The trip went well, with only a few recalculations. That is

until I approached New York City. Looking at the map, I thought I could "wing" it and, not listening to the GPS, made a wrong and crucial turn. The GPS woman's voice got increasingly demanding with her "recalculating, recalculating!" I was going entirely in the wrong direction. I knew I'd messed up when I passed by the Bronx Zoo. Uh, oh, I was in trouble. It was 5:00 in the evening, and I was driving in the middle of *Rush Hour Traffic* in New York City. As a small-town girl (pop. 4,000), I admit to a slight—let me be honest and say—a terrifying feeling of panic! I took a deep breath and prayed that God would guide my way. Knowing that God and the GPS voice knew precisely where I was, I focused on taking the right turns, trusting with blind faith that I could make my way through the maze of streets. And it was a maze! I briefly considered parking the rental car somewhere, calling a taxi, and finding Preston that way.

> Uhoh!

The GPS usually takes the shortest route, so I turned down side streets and one that looked like an alley! At one time, traffic stopped underneath the Lincoln Tunnel (no less), and the GPS kept saying, "recalculating, recalculating" because she had lost her signal! Her voice was so getting on my nerves. Now how was I supposed to turn around in the Lincoln Tunnel? As I made my way out of the tunnel, I noticed I was crossing over Interstate 95, a route that would take me out of New York City and back to Arkansas. I seriously thought about getting on I95 and not stopping until home. But long story short—I found Preston. I was never so glad to drive into that motel parking lot, praising and thanking God! I tell you what, I gave that big ole boy a huge kiss and a hug.

This end-of-life journey may look very similar. I've never traveled this road before, and I have no idea what is before me. Faith is stepping out into the unknown, believing that God is there to lead us to the other side. There may be some panicky voices from others, but I must listen to his still, quiet voice and trust him like a small child confidently taking my daddy's hand. At this point in my life, the only thing that I can do is trust that God knows exactly what he is doing and where he is taking me.

Traveling Toward Heaven

I know my God; I know I can trust him.

Here on earth, God does not force his people to do anything. He has given us free will. If we listen to his quiet, still voice, he's our heavenly GPS. He gives us directions, but it's up to us to follow them. He directs us to a different route when we make a wrong turn. He has hundreds of different paths for us to take when we go the wrong way, but ultimately all roads lead to the final destination. The way of the saved is Heaven, and the course of the unsaved is Hell. One thing that I do know is that Jesus is the only way to Heaven. Yes, he often allows us to travel different roads and gives us other choices as we go through life, but ultimately, God provides us with his HPS, Heavenly Positioning System. It's up to us to steer the car. In the HPS, there are no multiple roads to get to Heaven. There is only one way. Jesus is from Heaven, he came to Earth, and he went back to Heaven. He's the only one who knows the way. The world says, "Go this way, go this way." It can be so confusing. But listen to what Jesus says:

> There may be some panicky voices from others, but I must listen to God's still, quiet voice.

> "Don't let your hearts be troubled. Trust in God, and trust also in me. There is more than enough room in my Father's home. If this were not so, would I have told you that I am going to prepare a place for you? When everything is ready, I will come and get you, so that you will always be with me where I am. And you know the way to where I am going."

Thomas was so much like us. Even though he had walked daily with Jesus, he still didn't know the way.

"No, we don't know, Lord," Thomas said. "We have no idea where you are going, so how can we know the way?"

I can see the confusion on Thomas' face. He was so honest.

Jesus told him, "I am the way, the truth, and the life. *No one can come to the Father except through me. If you had really known me, you would know who my Father is. From now on, you do know him and have seen him!*" (John 14:1-7)

No one.
In today's world view, being exclusive is not okay. It's not okay to say Jesus is the only way to Heaven. If we believe Jesus was only a religious teacher, one of many through the centuries, then yes, it would be absurd to think that he is the only way. But Jesus didn't just speak about the truth; he is The Truth. Jesus is God himself. Being a Christ-follower is not an exclusive club reserved only for a few. In fact, Christianity is the most inclusive religion in the world. I heard a preacher from Fellowship Bible Church in Rogers, Arkansas, explain it this way: "Jesus is exclusive because there's only one way through him, but inclusive because everyone is invited. *There are no participation trophies into Heaven.*"[1]

> "There are no participation trophies into Heaven."

In the South, we would say, "Preach it, brother!"
I love how the *Message Bible* says it:

> This is how much God loved the world: He gave his Son, his one and only Son. And this is why: so that *no one* need be destroyed; by believing in him, anyone can have a whole and lasting life. God didn't go to all the trouble of sending his Son merely to point an accusing finger, telling the world how bad it was. He came to help, to put the world right again. (John 3:16)

No one.
Our world has gotten very small. We often rub shoulders with people of different religions. Each has a different view of God and how to get to Heaven.

Traveling Toward Heaven

Nancy Ortberg discussed this in her article "What Do Muslims Believe?"[2] In Islam, Allah is entirely incomprehensible. It is blasphemous to see Allah as someone who desires a relationship with us, a father and friend, and a God who prepares a place for us in Heaven. Allah doesn't want a relationship with his followers; he wants submission. The only way to know Allah's will is to pray ritual prayers five times daily. Contrast that to Jesus:

> "My command is this: Love each other as I have loved you. Greater love has no one than this: to lay down one's life for one's friends. You are my friends if you do what I command. I no longer call you servants because a servant does not know his master's business. Instead, I have called you friends, for everything that I learned from my Father I have made known to you." (John 15:12-15, NIV)

Islam requires rigorous adherence to good works. They believe that everyone is born sinless. By faithfully adhering to the words of Allah and Muhammad, they have unlimited potential. Their good works open the door to one of the seven levels of Heaven or Paradise. But they will one day be judged based on whether their good works outweigh their evil works. They have no way of knowing that Paradise is in their future. However, those who die as martyrs serving Allah are guaranteed a place in Paradise.

> "Do not say regarding those who are slain in the path of God that they are dead; rather they are alive, but you are not aware." Quran 2:154

> "Do not consider as dead those who are slain in the path of God; rather, they are alive and well-provided for in the presence of their Lord." Quran 3:169

Compare to Jesus:

> For it is by grace you have been saved, through faith—and

this is not from yourselves, it is the gift of God—not by works, so that no one can boast. (Ephesians 2:8, NIV)

There are different levels of Heaven in Islam. The highest is Paradise, and the lowest is Khuldi. The Christian Heaven and the Muslim Heaven are polar opposites. Paradise is like a garden (Jannah), where everything focuses on sensual pleasure—beautiful women, rich brocades, rivers of milk, honey, and wine. The Quran says:

> Other faces on that day shall be happy, well-pleased because of their striving, in a lofty garden, wherein you shall not hear vain talk. Therein is a fountain flowing, therein are thrones raised high, and drinking-cups ready placed, and cushions set in a row, and carpets spread out. (Surah 88:8-16)

Christians worship the one true and living God in Heaven. There is no marrying or emphasis on sensual pleasures as in the Quran. One day a group of Sadducees (who did not even believe in the afterlife) tried to trick Jesus by asking him about a woman whose husband(s) died. After each husband had died, she married his brother.

> "So, tell us, whose wife will she be in the resurrection?" For all seven were married to her. Jesus replied, "Your mistake is that you don't know the Scriptures, and you don't know the power of God. For when the dead rise, they will neither marry nor be given in marriage. In this respect, they will be like the angels in Heaven." (Matthew 22:28-30)

Can't you see the smoke coming out of their ears? There are no marrying multiple wives in Heaven. Also, what I love about this passage is that Jesus was speaking to a group of religious leaders who prided themselves in knowing the scriptures. He knew that they only read the Torah (the first five books of the Bible). He asked them a second time in Matthew 22:31, "Haven't you ever read about this in the scriptures? Long after Abraham, Isaac, and Jacob had died, God said, I *am* the God of Abraham, the God of Isaac, and the God of Jacob. So, he is the God of the LIVING, not the dead."

| Jesus—1 |
| Sadducees—0 |

In Hinduism, one can only obtain salvation (or moksha) after the worshiper is freed from the cycle of reincarnation and his spirit becomes one with his god. A person can only become free by eliminating bad karma—negative actions and intentions. The worshipper can free himself in four ways: selfless devotion, service to a particular god, understanding the universe, and mastering the steps needed to appease the gods fully. There are over a million gods, each with different paths to salvation. The worshiper desires to become one with their god by becoming a god—the original sin from the Garden of Eden.

Buddhism is even more complicated. A Buddhist doesn't believe in an omnipotent, omnipresent creator. Buddhists may pray to Buddha but don't believe he is divine. A Buddhist strives to attain salvation by attaining higher and higher states of being, the highest being Nirvana. When a Buddhist dies, the person is reincarnated into one of six realms: Heaven, human, animal, fighting a demon, hungry ghost, and Hell.

In Judaism, not everyone believes in Heaven. As I wrote earlier, Pharisees and Sadducees argued the concept of an afterlife for centuries. Today, most Reformed Jewish people (the least of the religious) don't believe in an afterlife. People only live on in the memories of their friends and family. The very religious (Orthodox) believe in Heaven, but the only way to get there is to do good works. The Conservative Jewish people (those in the middle) lean both ways—some toward the reformed side and some toward the orthodox side.

Traditional Judaism teaches that our bodies go to the grave after we die, but our souls go before God. One is assigned a place in Heaven depending on a merit system. Some believe those with uncleaned sins must go to Sheol for a while after they die. The soul stays in this temporary "Hell" for twelve months until it is released to go to *Olam Ha-Ba* (the World to Come). Others believe that the soul stays in Sheol until the Messiah comes.

Many other world religions have multiple ideas about how to achieve or not achieve the afterlife, everything from Scientology to Unitarian-Universalism. There's no getting around it; God has placed a hunger in our hearts to live forever.

> Yet God has made everything beautiful for its own time. He has planted eternity in the human heart, but even so, people cannot see the whole scope of God's work from beginning to end. (Ecclesiastics 3:11)

God created us to live forever with him, so he has also created a yearning for Heaven. He has provided the spiritual road map—the *TripTik*. (Remember those?) He wants *everyone* to choose salvation so that we might live forever. Over the centuries, people just got it wrong. Sin got in the way. How was God going to fix it? He decided to come down to earth, become a man, and show us the Way—the Only Way to him and the only Way to Heaven. He sent his son, Jesus, to take care of not just my sin but the sins of *all of mankind*. No, God is not exclusive. He wants every soul on earth to be with him and his son, Jesus. His voice is our (HPS) Heavenly Positioning System. If we listen to his voice and choose Jesus, we will find our way out of New York City into Heaven. God is waiting for us with open arms and a huge smile. I can't wait!

> His voice is our Heavenly Positioning System

> "It is he to whom and with whom we travel, and while he is at the end of our journey, he is also at every stopping place."[3]
> Elisabeth Elliot

Light-seeds

When life gets chaotic, and many voices are in your ear, how do you sort through those voices to hear God?

Jesus says if we trust him to lead us, we don't have to worry about knowing the right way. But—how are we like Thomas?

What does it mean: "There are no participation trophies in heaven?"

How can it be that Jesus is both exclusive and inclusive?

God has placed a hunger in our hearts to live forever. What does that mean to you?

Walk Me Into Heaven

6

The Spectators

I was just a spectator, looking through the lens of a camera and marveling. Men and women, young and old, of all body shapes and sizes, were getting ready for the day of their life. At least twelve to seventeen hours are ahead of them; grueling, tedious, never-ending, inspiring, unbearable, and remarkable.

They had trained for months for this one day. What must be going through their minds as they put on their wet suits, preparing to jump into the frigid water? There was no turning back now. What if they failed? Family members surrounded them with love and concern. Children looked with pride at their daddy or mama.

It was the Iron-man triathlon—a 2-mile swim, a 100-mile bike ride, and a 26-mile marathon. It was unthinkable. How was it even possible?

The sun rose golden over the water as 3,000 or more pink and green heads bobbed toward the race's starting point. As we leaned over the bridge to watch, we heard a loud cry, "Kayak, I need help." One man's race was over before it had begun.

Walk Me Into Heaven

For the rest of the long day, we followed the different legs of the race, placing ourselves at just the right vantage point to get the best fleeting view of our two athletes. We followed their progress based on an app that showed us where they were at any point in the race. Then we watched and waited. "There he is!" Cameras up, we waved and shouted encouragement as he rode by. One group had T-shirts that said, "Wait, wait, CHEER, wait, wait!"

As the day wore on and the 26-mile marathon run began, we could see the fatigue and determination etched on their faces. Sometimes family members or friends would run a short distance with them, shouting encouragement. Several times I saw an athlete stop, kiss his wife or child, and keep running; tears streaming down his face. Close by, a little girl shouted in a high thin voice, "Daddy, you have to finish!"

Around 8:00 that night, we made our way to the finish line. People crowded up and down the final raceway, encouraging the exhausted racers. Some could barely make it, just putting one foot in front of the other and leaning toward the finish line. Others had a burst of speed, wanting to finish strong. Completely depleted, their faces still shown with joy. They had finished! We were so proud of them.

It was a surreal day, taking many of us, athletes and spectators, into a place we had never been. I thought about this day as we traveled back home. How much like life this is: preparation, difficulty, pain, endurance, joy, patience, discouragement, encouragement, relief—and finally—the finish line. We may get there at different times, but we will all finish. God is there with all who have gone before us, cheering us on and welcoming us into eternal life.

> We may get there at different times, but we will all finish.

Shortly after I returned home, I read this: "With the three divine Persons will be all those who have gone before us, delighted that we have finally arrived. In this life, we often feel like lonely marathon runners, but then we will emerge into a great

54

The Spectators

stadium with an immense crowd rising to applaud us. Surely then we will fall on our knees and cry, but our tears will be tears of joy, not sadness. God will take us by the hand and present us to the gathered community where everyone is totally on our side."[1]

It's well worth the training--2,658 started the day, and 2,517 finished.

> Therefore, since we are surrounded by such a huge crowd of witnesses to the life of faith, let us strip off every weight that slows us down, especially the sin that so easily trips us up. And let us run with endurance the race God has set before us. We do this by keeping our eyes on Jesus, the champion who initiates and perfects our faith. Because of the joy awaiting him, he endured the cross, disregarding its shame. Now he is seated in the place of honor beside God's throne. Think of all the hostility he endured from sinful people; then you won't become weary and give up. After all, you have not yet given your lives in your struggle against sin. (Hebrews 12:1-4)

As we draw toward the end of the race, it's encouraging to know that we are surrounded by a vast crowd (or cloud, NIV) of witnesses who shout encouragement to us as we "strengthen our feeble arms and weak knees" (Hebrews 12:12). I found out that the Greek word, *nephos*, translated as clouds, has an additional meaning. The ancient Greeks used the word *nephos*, or clouds, to describe the highest seats in the bleachers of a stadium. Can't you see them? All those saints from Hebrews 11, like Abel, Enoch, Noah, Abraham, and Sarah, are standing up on the highest rows of the stadium, cheering us to the top of their lungs on to the end. Back then, witnesses meant the same thing as they do now—a watcher who has seen the evidence with their own eyes. Yes, they have experienced victory. They know the joy that awaits us in the end. No wonder they're cheering. We are not trying to impress them, however. We run

Can't you see them?

our race for Jesus and Jesus alone.

I'm writing this chapter at the end of December. My husband and I have been watching football bowl game after bowl game. If you've watched football or any sport for any period, you understand how intense the crowd can get. Okay, that word just doesn't cut it. Ardent, enthusiastic, fervent, vehement, zealous? When a team wins, the fans are exultant, elated, triumphant, "over the moon," and never to be sad again. The cameramen love zooming into the faces of the people witnessing their team's touchdown or victory. Pure joy! They're hugging each other, jumping up and down, giving high-fives—going crazy. But then the camera zooms over to the other side. Here there is gnashing of teeth. People are crying, holding their arms above their heads, unbelieving and distraught. What words describe this? Anguish, heartache, misery, disconsolation, bummer—you get the picture. In the championship playoff last week, there were only a few seconds left to kick a field goal and win the game. He missed. You can only imagine what that young man was feeling. Unfortunately, people will discuss that missed field goal for the next twenty years. They don't forget these things.

If you have lived long enough, you have probably been a spectator to the death of a loved one. This quote from John Rice (evangelist and editor of the *Sword of the Lord*) said it bluntly:

"We Christians often act like heathens. We preach that it is wonderful to be a Christian, that Heaven is to be gained and Hell shunned. Then when one of our loved ones dies, we act as if it were all a lie. Our actions say that this world is better than the next, that death is a tragedy, and we ask querulously in our unbelief, Why? Why? Why?... Shame on us!

When we weep and lament at the death of our loved ones [beyond God's-honoring grief], we often make void our testimony, cast reflection upon the Bible, and irreverence on

> "We Christians often act like heathens."

The Spectators

Heaven. For the Christian, death is not a tragedy but a glorious promotion – not the sad end, but the glorious beginning."[2]

Okaaaay. That was blunt. People back then weren't afraid to say what they thought, were they?

It is tough to lose a loved one before their time, but the death of a Christ-follower at the end of their days is difficult, also. I believe that the death of an older saint should be a time of love and comfort and then a time of celebration and rejoicing. But no matter how old our loved one is, we still grieve. That's natural. God designed the grief process in us to psychologically work through the loss of someone we love. Jesus said, "Blessed are those who mourn, for they will be comforted." Even he cried when Lazarus died.

As spectators, we have a role to play. Paul writing to his young friend Timothy says:

> As for me, my life has already been poured out as an offering to God. The time of my death is near. I have fought the good fight, I have finished the race, and I have remained faithful. And now the prize awaits me—the crown of righteousness, which the Lord, the righteous Judge, will give me on the day of his return. And the prize is not just for me but for all who eagerly look forward to his appearing. (2 Timothy 4:6-8)

But before that happens, Paul asks:

> Timothy, please come as soon as you can. Demas has deserted me because he loves the things of this life and has gone to Thessalonica. Crescens has gone to Galatia, and Titus has gone to Dalmatia. Only Luke is with me. Bring Mark with you when you come, for he will be helpful to me in my ministry. (2 Timothy 4:9-11)

This scripture always gets to me. Paul does not want to be

alone in the end. He asks Timothy to come, and "When you come, be sure to bring the coat I left with Carpus at Troas. Also, bring my books, and especially my papers" (2 Timothy 4:13).

Paul was cold; he needed his coat and his friends to be with him at the end. He wanted to make sure that his house was in order. I can imagine that as those gathered around him, he gave those books and papers to them.

Just as I wrote at the beginning of this chapter, God has a vital role for spectators on the saint's end-of-life journey. We are there to cheer, encourage, and hold on to our loved one until he (or she) crosses the finish line. We are there to give support and, even when there's pain, to just "be there." Sometimes the race to the end is a sprint, and sometimes, it's a marathon, especially for

> "Do your best to get here before winter."
> —2 Timothy 4:21

those of you who have family members with Alzheimer's disease or other kinds of dementia. It's so difficult to watch them suffer. But where would they be without us? The tragedy of Covid was all the saints who died in their hospital beds without their family holding their hands. God did not leave or forsake them, but it was difficult for the families.

Then there were the ultimate spectators, Mary, John, Mary Magdalene, and perhaps a few other unnamed women. Mary, the mother of Jesus, witnessed her son's horrific crucifixion and death. I cannot even imagine watching my son suffer and die like that. She didn't have to be at the foot of the cross. But no matter what, she wouldn't let him go through that without her. In pain, she brought him into the world. In pain, she would help him leave. Thankfully, she wasn't alone. Even though her other sons and daughters weren't there with her, we know that John and Mary Magdalene stood by her side. Mary Magdalene's words from my book, *To See Him Face to Face*:

> We were there for him. We stood among the mocking crowd along the Via Dolorosa. We watched as he struggled through the streets, bleeding and torn, a crown of

The Spectators

thorns on his head. We wanted to go out there and lift that cross from his shoulders! We watched from a distance as they pounded the nails into his hands and feet, flinching with each blow of the hammer. We held our breath as we heard his screams of pain when they lifted him high into the air.

John joined us. Of all the men, John was the only one with the courage to be at Golgotha, where Jesus was crucified. We all wanted to shield Mary from the pain. How could she stand there and watch her son suffer? As she had endured the pains of childbirth, she now had to endure the excruciating pain of his death.

I felt like I was back in the same suffocating cave of darkness that I had been in before Jesus delivered me. The light of day began to grow dim.

"Oh, God!" I cried out as I fell to my knees. "God, take away his pain. Don't forsake him! God help me!"

The light of day turned into darkness.

"Mary," a voice said. I felt the touch of a hand on my shoulder.

"Mary, it's over. He's gone."

It was John's voice I heard. He began gathering all of us together. I looked toward the cross. The sky was lightening now with the sun setting in the west, silhouetting the cross and Jesus' lifeless body.

Mary and her friends had no idea what was about to happen. Here is Mary Magdalene after encountering the resurrected Jesus at the tomb:

I didn't want to leave him again—to let him out of my sight. I tried to hold on to him and never let go.

"Go now, Mary," he urged gently. "I will never leave your or forsake you again. I will be with you always."

Reluctantly, I left him. When I turned and looked one more time, he was gone. Suddenly, the realization of what truly happened bubbled inside me, and I ran to share my good news.

Jesus Christ is alive! I saw him——I talked to him! Of all people, he chose me to be the one to have the privilege of sharing the Good News!

When I burst into the house with my news, Mary was there. She sat in a chair by the door, her hands folded serenely on her lap, waiting. I walked over to her and knelt. Taking her hands in mine, I said, "Mary, I saw him!" Tears of joy began running down her cheeks.

"He is alive?" she whispered. I smiled and nodded at her.

I looked around at all the stunned faces of those gathered around us. Still holding Mary's hand, I stood up and declared, "He spoke to me. He said to tell you that he was ascending to his Father and your Father, his God, and your God. But he wants to see you first!"[3]

These precious women were spectators to his death, but most importantly for us:

> They were witnesses to his Resurrection!

Can you imagine? Someday, that will be us.

The Spectators

Light-seeds

Truth: We may arrive at different times, but we will all finish. Can you imagine your finish line?

Who are you running the race to impress?

What do you think of John Rice's quote: "We Christians often act like heathens."

Paul was not reluctant to ask his friends to stand with him to the end. Who will be there for you? Can pride get in the way?

Jesus did not go to the cross alone. As you stand beside a loved one on their journey to Heaven, how can God use you?

Walk Me Into Heaven

# 7

The Hard Chapter or
(What Keeps You Out of Heaven)

"When I get to Heaven, I shall see three wonders there. The first wonder will be to see many people there whom I did not expect to see; the second wonder will be to miss many people whom I did expect to see; and the third and greatest wonder of all will be to find myself there."[1]

—John Newton

Okay. Okay. Okay. It has been fun writing this book so far, but way back in the distant recesses of my brain (where I conveniently place things I don't want to think about) is the thought that I have yet to tell all the story. Who goes to Heaven? What keeps you out of Heaven? Is Hell a real place? I need to address these things before I move on.

In Chapter One, I wrote about how we can know Jesus. How to be "saved." So—what are we saved from? Death and separation from God.

> For the wages of sin is death, but the free gift of God is eternal life through Christ Jesus our Lord. (Romans 6:23)

C.S. Lewis once wrote about Hell:
"There is no doctrine which I would more willingly remove from Christianity than this if it lay in my power. But it has the full support of Scripture and, especially, of Our Lord's own words; it has always been held by Christendom; and it has the support of reason. If a game is played, it must be possible to lose it.[2]

If my Razorbacks are playing in an important football or baseball game, I like to record the game and watch it after knowing whether they win or lose. A lot less stressful that way! (Actually, I don't watch them again if they lose.) The good news about Christianity is that Jesus gave us a way (The Way) to confidently know how to win the game without a shadow of a doubt.

But he also talked a lot—a lot about the losers. There are many scriptures in the gospels in which Jesus talks about Hell. Jesus doesn't talk about Hell to frighten us, but he loves us and gives us a way to escape it. He wants us to live forever with him and not apart from him.

Tim Keller tweeted this in 2021: "Unless you believe in Hell (the place of God's absence), you will never know how much Jesus loves you and what he went through for you."[3]

Jesus did not hesitate to talk about eternal punishment or Hell. I'm sure that I skipped over those scriptures when I read the gospel because I didn't want to think about it. I grew up in a church that never mentioned Hell or Heaven, for that matter. Maybe the church was trying to get past the old "hellfire and brimstone" theology blasted from the pulpits during the 18th and 19th centuries. Jonathan Edwards' "Sinners in the Hand of an Angry God" sermon was said to be so compelling and convincing that hearers could smell the sulfur burning. Edwards felt it was his responsibility to warn people of the reality of Hell. Still, he also emphasized the mercy of God.[4] A.W. Tozer summed it up by saying: "Death fixes the status of the man who loved his sins, and he is sent to the place of the rejected where there is for him no further hope. That is Hell, and it may be well we know so little about it. What we do know is sufficiently terrifying."[5]

The Hard Chapter or *(What Keeps You Out of Heaven)*

As a young mother, I often warned my children of the world's dangers, not to be overly dramatic, but to point out the obvious. Don't run with a knife in your hand. Imagine what would happen. Look both ways before you cross the street. Imagine what would happen if you didn't. Don't play with matches. What if the house caught on fire? Don't pet a stray dog. What would it feel like to be bitten by that dog? Don't get in a car with strangers. When my kids and grandkids turned sixteen and began to drive, I reminded them to buckle up. Don't text and drive. Think what could happen! I didn't hesitate to draw a picture of what might happen if my children disobeyed. In scripture, Jesus explains Hell in the same way. Sometimes we need a picture. In Luke 16, Jesus tells the story of Lazarus and the rich man.

> Imagine what would happen.

The rich man shouted, "Father Abraham, have some pity! Send Lazarus over here to dip the tip of his finger in water and cool my tongue. I am in anguish in these flames." (Luke 16:24)

If your hand causes you to sin, cut it off. It's better to enter eternal life with only one hand than to go into the unquenchable fires of hell. (Mark 9:43)

Just as the weeds are sorted out and burned in the fire, so it will be at the end of the world. The Son of Man will send his angels, and they will remove from his Kingdom everything that causes sin and all who do evil. And the angels will throw them into the fiery furnace, where there will be weeping and gnashing of teeth. Then the righteous will shine like the sun in their Father's Kingdom. Anyone with ears to hear should listen and understand! (Matthew 13:40-43)

There's no doubt that Jesus taught the reality of Hell vividly and memorably so that we are not unaware of the consequences of sin. People often ask, "Why would a loving God allow suffering in this world?" or "Why would a righteous God allow the Putins and Hitlers to cause so much evil?" God will not let evil prevail forever. He will make it right. In his classic, *Knowing God,* J. I. Packer writes of the goodness and severity of God:

> "The character of God is the guarantee that all wrongs will be righted someday; when the 'day of God's wrath, when his righteous judgment will be revealed' (Romans 2:5) arrives, retribution will be exact, and no problems of cosmic unfairness will remain to haunt us. God is the Judge so that justice will be done."[6]

We often say self-righteously, "Yay, God, go get them!" But remember Jesus saying:

> "And why worry about a speck in your friend's eye when you have a log in your own? How can you think of saying to your friend, 'Let me help you get rid of that speck in your eye,' when you can't see past the log in your own eye? Hypocrite! First, get rid of the log in your own eye; then you will see well enough to deal with the speck in your friend's eye." (Matthew 7:3-5)

God will not let evil prevail forever.

Oh yeah, God has his way of bringing things home, doesn't he? The world is always talking about "social justice," but unfortunately, this is far and away what Biblical justice is all about. We are all fallen, no matter our race or creed. We all fall short of the glory of God. The Bible states that God is not a respecter of persons (Romans 2:11). God does not deal with us by the color of our skin or whether we are American, Irish, African, Norwegian, male, female, rich, or poor. God looks past all of that. He looks at the heart. The only "identity" that will be important to him is whether we are "in Christ" or not.

> No one is righteous—not even one. No one is truly wise; no one is seeking God. All have turned away; all have be-

The Hard Chapter or *(What Keeps You Out of Heaven)*

come useless. No one does good, not a single one. (Romans 3:10-12)

Well—there you go. God does not hold back the truth. But he is also full of grace and love, not wanting anyone to perish. I love the way the Message Bible says it:

> Don't overlook the obvious here, friends. With God, one day is as good as a thousand years, a thousand years as a day. God isn't late with his promise as some measure lateness. He is restraining himself on account of you, holding back the End because *he doesn't want anyone lost.* He's giving everyone space and time to change. (2 Peter 3:9, Message)

> God looks at the heart.

He doesn't want anyone lost.
Jesus could have come back to earth centuries ago, but he keeps waiting—restraining himself because he wants everyone to have the chance to believe in him. I focused on the word "everyone." I've been trying to understand the Biblical meaning of *equality* and *equity*. These words are bantered about in society and politics today. Seeing the difference is essential as they apply to Heaven or Hell. As far as equality goes, we are all equal-opportunity sinners. It doesn't matter if we were born in the most Christian homes or dens of iniquity; we all need repentance and faith in Jesus.

Sheila Lewine, in her blog, *The Way of the Word,* wrote a post entitled, *God's View of Equality and Equity.*

> "God is also a God of equity. The same outcome applies to everyone based on a simple decision to accept or reject His gift of salvation. You see, in the world's eyes, equity means you need something extra to achieve a result, or you need less of something to get to the same outcome. In God's economy, no one earns anything – salvation is a gift, by grace alone, through faith alone

in Jesus Christ. The results are exactly the same for everyone. Those who willingly choose to accept the gift spend eternity in Heaven. Those who willingly reject spend eternity in Hell."[7]

Billy Graham was asked this question:

"I heard someone say the other day that when we get to Heaven, we're probably going to be surprised at some of the people who will be there. Do you think it's true?" His answer: "Yes, I believe it is true (and so, incidentally, did my wife, Ruth, who often quoted this statement). But we also may be surprised when we get to Heaven to discover who isn't there!"[8]

> "In God's economy, no one earns anything—salvation is a gift." SL

Many stories in the gospels show God's grace even to the end because he doesn't want anyone to perish. In Matthew 20:1-16, Jesus tells the parable of the workers. Some worked all day, some worked half a day, and some only worked a few hours. Each man received the same wage when they lined up at the end of the day. "But that's not fair!" The first two grumbled, "We worked all day and received the same pay as this yokel who only worked a few hours!"

> He replied to the one speaking for the rest, "Friend, I haven't been unfair. We agreed on the wage of a dollar, didn't we? So, take it and go. I decided to give to the one who came last, the same as you. Can't I do what I want with my own money? Are you going to get stingy because I am generous?"
>
> Here it is again, the Great Reversal: many of the first ending up last, and the last first. (Matthew 20:13-16, Message)

In Ezekiel 18, God says:
"But if a wicked person turns away from the wickedness they have committed and does what is just and right, they will save their life. Because they consider all the offenses they have

The Hard Chapter or *(What Keeps You Out of Heaven)*

committed and turn away from them, that person will surely live; they will not die. Yet the Israelites say, 'The way of the Lord is not just.' Are my ways unjust, people of Israel? Is it not your ways that are unjust?'" (Ezekiel 18:27-29, NIV)

And then, there were the thieves who hung on both sides of Jesus. In their agony, both men heard Jesus say: "Father, forgive them for they do not know what they are doing" (Luke 23:34, NIV). They heard people scoff, "You saved others, Jesus. Now save yourself!" One thief hurled insults at Jesus along with the crowd. "So, you're the Messiah, are you? Prove it by saving yourself—and us, too, while you're at it" (Luke 23:39). The other thief—what was going through his mind? Finally—finally, at the very end of his life, his heart was touched by Jesus. At the very last minute, he believed. He knew. He yelled over at his friend:

> "Don't you fear God even when you have been sentenced to die? We deserve to die for our crimes, but this man hasn't done anything wrong."

Humbly, with probably his last gasping breath, he said,

> "Jesus, remember me when you come into your kingdom." And Jesus replied, *"I assure you,* today you will be with me in paradise." (Luke 23:40-43)

"I assure you." This man was a thief, a sinner, a man destined for Hell, to be separated from God and forever lost. This man had probably not set foot in a Temple in years. He had turned his back on God. Did he have a mother somewhere praying for him? Did he have a wife who never gave up hope? Somehow, however, he ended up crucified beside our Lord. He walked into Heaven with Jesus. Yesterday, our pastor shared a clip from a sermon by Allistar Beggs, pastor of Parkside Church in Cleveland, Ohio. The story was of the thief on the cross. When he got to Heaven, the angel asked him all kinds of theological questions about his

life. The man couldn't answer any of them. Finally, in frustration, the angel threw up his hands and asked one final question, "On what basis are you here?" The thief said, "The man in the middle said I can come."[9] It's not about us, it's about what Jesus did for us on the cross.

Don't ever give up hope on someone. Keep praying. Keep believing. Keep showing them God's unfailing love. It's never too late to repent and accept God's gift of salvation.

However, here's the thing. We don't know when we will take our last breath. Don't wait. Please don't put it off. Don't take a chance. Salvation is free; it will make a difference for eternity and every day of your life. You won't regret it.

> "The man in the middle said I could come." AB

I think back on Billy Graham's quote about being surprised when we get to Heaven about who is and isn't there. Remember, there's a difference between believing in Jesus and having a relationship with him. Even the demons believe and tremble in terror (James 2:19). Jesus once said this:

> "Not everyone who says to me, 'Lord, Lord,' will enter the kingdom of Heaven, but only the one who does the will of my Father who is in Heaven. Many will say to me on that day, 'Lord, Lord, did we not prophesy in your name and in your name drive out demons and, in your name, perform many miracles?' Then I will tell them plainly, 'I never knew you. Away from me, you evildoers!'" (Matthew 7:21-23, NIV)

Think of Judas, who walked with Jesus, cast out demons, and even performed miracles but never really "knew" him. It's all about our hearts and willingness to lay aside our own "truths" and walk in His Truth. The thief on the cross never walked one step with Jesus, but his heart was open to him, and that's what he requires of us. He doesn't expect us to be perfect; Heaven help us (literally)! He wants a relationship with us. How? Talk

The Hard Chapter or *(What Keeps You Out of Heaven)*

to him (prayer). Read his words (the Bible). Do what he says. (Live your life for him.)

> This is the testimony in essence:
> *God gave us eternal life; the life is in his Son.*
> *So, whoever has the Son, has life;*
> *whoever rejects the Son rejects life.*
> (1 John 5:11, 12, Message)

Remember this: Eternal life is not a reward but a gift.

No eye has seen, no ear has heard,
and no mind has imagined
what God has prepared
for those who love him. (1 Corinthians 2:9)

Okay. That's settled. Let's get on to the good part!

Light-seeds

Does it bother you that Jesus talks about Hell as much or more than Heaven?

"God will not allow evil to prevail forever." Does that give you peace?

What identity is important to God? Those in the world or those in Jesus?

Is it a comfort to you that God does not want anyone lost?

How do you understand equality and equity in reference to Heaven?

What does this mean to you in today's world? "In God's economy, no one earns anything—salvation is a gift."

"It's not about us—it's what Jesus did on the cross." Have you grasped that simple truth?

8

Good News, Silas! You Were Right!

It was ten years ago. My daughter called to tell me a delightful story. She had put her two boys, ages 4 and 7, down for the night. They watched a G-rated TV show that day where the father in the story died of a heart attack. It must have got them thinking like little boys are prone to do—especially those two! Wide awake in their bunks, they started talking about Heaven. I wish I had been a fly on the wall that night, listening in on this theological conversation, because soon after, the youngest, Slaton, came out and said, "Silas says that you can do everything you want to in Heaven! Is that true?" Their mom looked at him and said, "Yes, Slaton, that's right. It's a really great place!" Satisfied, Slaton padded back to bed. When he returned to the room, his mama heard him say, "Good news, Silas! You were right!"

Shortly after that, a wonderful father in our community died of cancer. Diagnosed two weeks before I was, we went through chemo together. This man and his wife shared their faith journey with the entire community. They expected a miracle. The miracle happened in Heaven. On the front page of the bulletin for his Celebration of Life service was a picture of Chris standing confidently on the beach with these words, "Today, I am not only surviving, I am thriving."

I don't understand why I'm still here twelve years later, and Chris is in Heaven. I admit to being honest with God and asking Him "why"? We often don't have a "God perspective" when losing people we love. We need help understanding.

> "For my thoughts are not your thoughts,
> neither are your ways my ways,"
> declares the Lord.
> "As the Heavens are higher than the earth,
> so are my ways higher than your ways
> and my thoughts than your thoughts.
> There will come a time when we understand."
> (Isaiah 55:8, 9, NIV)

In the last chapter of John, Jesus told Peter: "When you are old, you will stretch out your hands, and others will dress you and take you where you don't want to go" (John 21:18, NLT). Peter responded in his typically honest way:

> Turning his head, Peter noticed the disciple Jesus loved following right behind. When Peter noticed him, he asked Jesus, "Master, what's going to happen to *him*?"
> Jesus said, "If I want him to live until I come again, what's that to you? You—follow me." That is how the rumor got out among the brothers that this disciple wouldn't die. But that is not what Jesus said. He simply said, "If I want him to live until I come again, what's that to you?" (John 21:20-23, Message).

At Chris' service, the minister read these words:

> "Don't let your hearts be troubled. Trust in God, and trust also in me. There is more than enough room in my Father's home. If this were not so, would I have told you that I am

Good News, Silas! You Were Right!

going to prepare a place for you? When everything is ready, I will come and get you, so that you will always be with me where I am. And you know the way to where I am going." (John 14:1-4)

The good news is that, yes, Silas, you were right! My friend, Chris, is in Heaven, a more wonderful place than we could ever imagine. Given a choice, he would never change places with me. He is right where he wants to be. When God is ready for me, I'll be ready for him.

Can we do everything we want to do in Heaven? All I know is that Jesus has prepared a place for us—a good place. If we are with him, then yes, we will be doing everything we want to do because it will be a place that fulfills every possible need that we might have to serve him for all eternity. Jesus said that he wouldn't tell us this unless it was true. There will come a time when we are all gathered with Christ, living the eternal life he has planned for us. It's all in God's timing.

Here's what I have learned: Yes, Heaven is real, but the miracle

> Someday everything that I love here on earth will be completely restored.

of the resurrection tells me that someday everything that I love here on earth will be restored completely—there will be a new Heaven and a new earth. I glance up from my laptop to see the most glorious sunrise. The muted early morning sky is a robin's egg blue. Iridescent peach clouds swirl across the sky, lined with a soft white border. The limbs of the trees bob up and down as squirrels scamper in between the branches and birds hop from limb to limb. It's so pretty. Winter has just begun. The lawn is burnt toast, and dead plants fill my once beautiful and colorful pots, but the sky reminds me that God is in his Heaven and someday spring will come. We will worship him forever and ever and ever . . .

Heaven! That's what the remainder of this book is about. I have spent hours researching everything I could find about Heaven. As I said initially, Randy Alcorn inspired me with his book

Heaven. This book caught my attention, for sure! It encouraged me to think about the future with the Lord in new and exciting ways. I wanted to learn all I could learn about this magnificent place. I can't wait to share it with you.

Dwight L Moody was a well-known evangelist in the 19th century who revolutionized evangelism in the United States. He was a man of prayer whose sermon texts always came from the Bible. He said this about Heaven:

> "Surely it is not wrong for us to think and talk about Heaven. I like to find out all I can about it. I expect to live there through all eternity. If I were going to dwell in any place in this country, if I were going to make it my home, I would inquire about its climate, about the neighbors I would have – about everything, in fact, that I could learn concerning it. If soon you were going to emigrate, that is the way you would feel. Well, we are all going to emigrate in a very little while. We are going to spend eternity in another world... Is it not natural that we should look and listen and try to find out who is already there and what is the route to take?"[1]

> "Surely it is not wrong for us to think and talk about Heaven." DM

Over the centuries, Christians have pictured Heaven in various ways. Some see us sitting on a cloud, strumming a harp for all eternity. Not very exciting to think about, is it? Where did we get this idea? Cartoons, books, and movies have pushed this concept to the point that most Christians have no idea what God has in store for us in Heaven. Who would want to live for all eternity in a disembodied existence in a non-physical Heaven? Is Heaven a never-ending worship service in the sky? Maria Shriver wrote a children's book called *What's Heaven?* She writes: "Heaven is a beautiful place where you can sit on soft clouds and talk. If you're good throughout your life, you get to go [there]..."[2] Maria's words are not only unscriptural but also—wrong.

76

Good News, Silas! You Were Right!

In a *Time Magazine* article entitled *Christians Wrong About Heaven*, N.T. (Tom) Wright states:

"Greek-speaking Christians influenced by Plato saw our cosmos as shabby and misshapen and full of lies, and the idea was not to make it right but to escape it and leave behind our material bodies. The church at its best has always come back toward the Hebrew view, but there have been times when the Greek view was very influential."[3]

Likewise, in his popular book, *All Things New: Heaven, Earth, and the Restoration of Everything You Love,* pastor John Eldredge laments:

"Everybody I talk to still has these anemic, wispy views of Heaven, as a place up there somewhere, where we go to attend the eternal-worship-service-in-the-sky. Instead, the renewal of all things simply means that the earth you love—all your special places and treasured memories—is restored, renewed, and given back to you."[4]

I have so many questions. Sometimes I think that I understand, and then it slips away. Kind of like the evasive answer to an algebraic equation—entirely beyond me. Paul says it perfectly:

> Now we see things imperfectly, like puzzling reflections in a mirror, but then we will see everything with perfect clarity. (In Greek, face to face.) All that I know now is partial and incomplete, but then I will know everything completely, just as God now knows me completely. (1 Corinthians 13:12)

Or in Cindy's Version (CV):

> "I'm squinting and trying so hard to visualize all of this, but I know at some point it will all come into focus. I only have a small part of the puzzle, but my God, who knows me completely inside and out, will show everything to me someday."

> I'm squinting.

I am extremely nearsighted and have been since childhood.

Walk Me Into Heaven

Without my glasses, everything in the distance is blurry and indistinguishable. Here's the good thing: if you're nearsighted, you can see close-up well. Christians are spiritually nearsighted, we can see things right before our noses, but the future or in the distance is blurry. As a preteen, I hated my glasses. (Think brown cat-eyed frames with thick lenses.) I realized that if I squinted and narrowed my eyes, I could usually make out something far off. I would do this all the time when I saw a group of friends walking ahead of me. I could tell who they were by their shape and gait. My mother would notice me squinting and say, "Cindy, put on your glasses!" With myopic spiritual eyes, we squint toward Heaven and guess what's ahead. I like how the *Message Bible* says it:

> We don't yet see things clearly. We're squinting in a fog, peering through a mist. But it won't be long before the weather clears, and the sun shines bright! We'll see it all then, see it all as clearly as God sees us, knowing him directly just as he knows you! (1 Corinthians 13:12)

Even though our spiritual eyes are often myopic, God says, "It won't be long!" In the meantime, I can hear him say, "Cindy, put on your brown, cat-eyed glasses. I've got something for you to see."

He also gives us his light. We can follow a lighted path even if we can't see clearly.

> "Your word is a lamp to guide my feet and a light for my path." (Psalm 119:105)

In the remainder of this book, I want us to walk the lighted path of God's Word, put on our spiritual glasses, and see some things we've never seen before. God has a lot to show us in his Word about eternity. I have so many questions. Some questions I will cover in the rest of the book—and the others? I will continue to chew on them.

- What happens immediately after we die?

Good News, Silas! You Were Right!

- What are the differences between the Heaven we go to when we die and the Heaven we live in on the new earth?
- Will we be asleep until the resurrection of the body?
- What did Jesus mean when he said: "Today you will be with me in Paradise?"
- Will I be in Heaven when Jesus comes back? Will he come back to a new Heaven and a new earth? Are there two different Heavens?

Relationship with God:
- Will we be able to talk to God face to face?
- How does everyone have access to Jesus at the same time?
- What kind of relationship will we have with angels?
- Why does God want us in Heaven with him for all eternity?

Physical Body
- What kind of body will we have in Heaven?
- Will we be young again?
- Can we walk through walls like Jesus?
- Where in the world will all those people live?
- Will we eat in Heaven?
- Will we have evil thoughts or feelings in Heaven? Will we sin?
- What about cremation?
- Will we know all things in Heaven?
- Will we sleep in Heaven?
- Will we have our own house in Heaven?

What will we do for all eternity?
- Will Heaven be boring?
- Will there be sports, art, or culture in Heaven?
- Can we sing in the Heavenly Choir?
- Can we travel anywhere in the universe?

Relationships with others
- Whom will we meet in Heaven?
- What kind of relationship will I have with my husband? My family?
- Will I get to meet my great, great, great—grandparents? What questions would I ask of them?

- Will people recognize us in Heaven?
- Can people look down from Heaven at us?

What will Heaven look like?
- Will there be clocks or calendars in Heaven? Days and nights? Seasons?
- Where is Heaven located?
- Is Heaven a place we will recognize, or will it be someplace beyond our earthly comprehension?
- Will the new earth be like the old?
- Are there streets of gold? Pearly gates? Jeweled walls?

Animals
- Are there animals in Heaven? Pets?

Reigning with Jesus
- What does it mean to reign with Christ?
- Are there different rewards in Heaven? Will we care?
- Will we rule with Christ? What does that even look like?

Whew! Lord, I have so many questions! Please help me understand.

Good News, Silas! You Were Right!

Light-seeds

Jesus told Peter: "When you are old, you will stretch out your hands, and others will dress you and take you where you don't want to go." When Peter asked him about John, Jesus said, "If I want him to live until I come again, what's that to you? You—follow me." Does that give you peace, or does that make you uncomfortable?

Dwight L. Moody said, "Surely it's not wrong for us to talk about Heaven." Why do you think people shy away from talking about Heaven?

How have people gotten it wrong about Heaven?

What questions do you have about Heaven?

Walk Me Into Heaven

9

Sore Puzzler or *(I'm So Confused)*

I admit it. Sometimes I feel like the Grinch. "I puzzle and puzzle 'till my puzzler is sore." There is so much that I have wondered about Heaven. So many questions. I read someone's commentary or scripture and think, "Yes! That's it." Then, I read someone else's commentary and think, "No—maybe that's it."

The early church must have had all kinds of questions, also. "What do you think, Paul? You tell us all about Jesus. You say he came back to life. You say that the disciples and all those people saw him—alive. Then the disciples saw him go up into Heaven, even. What does that mean to us, Paul? What about our friends who have died? Where are they?"

> And regarding the question, friends, that has come up about what happens to those already dead and buried, we don't want you in the dark any longer. First off, you must not carry on over them like people who have nothing to look forward to, as if the grave were the last word. Since Jesus died and broke loose from the grave, God will most certainly bring

back to life those who died in Jesus.

And then this:

> We can tell you with complete confidence—we have the Master's word on it—that when the Master comes again to get us, those of us who are still alive will not get a jump on the dead and leave them behind. In actual fact, they'll be ahead of us. The Master himself will give the command. Archangel thunder! God's trumpet blast! He'll come down from Heaven, and the dead in Christ will rise—they'll go first. Then the rest of us who are still alive at the time will be caught up with them into the clouds to meet the Master. Oh, we'll be walking on air! And then there will be one huge family reunion with the Master. So, reassure one another with these words. (1 Thessalonians 4:13-18, Message)

> **Is it too good to be true? Wishful thinking?**

Is it too good to be true? Wishful thinking? Pie in the sky? Fool's paradise? So many things in life that we have put our hopes and dreams in turn out to be a bust. But Revelation tells us it's true.

> And the one sitting on the throne said, "Look, I am making everything new!" And then he said to me, "Write this down, for what I tell you is trustworthy and true." (Revelation 21:5)

How do we know it's true? Because God has staked his reputation on his Word. He is "the Alpha and the Omega, the beginning and the end" (Revelation 21:6). I believe him.

Here's my question: where do we go when we take our last breath? When we talk about Grandmom being in "Heaven," where is that? What is the difference between the present (or intermediate) Heaven and the eternal Heaven? I have learned so much about Heaven, and it is so exciting! Let's discuss the

Sore Puzzler or *(I'm So Confused)*

intermediate Heaven.

In his blog on Heaven, Randy Alcorn explains it this way: "Books on Heaven often fail to distinguish between the intermediate and eternal states, using the one word—Heaven—as all-inclusive. But this is an important distinction. The present Heaven is a temporary lodging, a waiting place (a delightful one!) until the return of Christ and our bodily resurrection. The eternal Heaven, the New Earth, is our true home, the place where we will live forever with our Lord and each other. The great redemptive promises of God will find their ultimate fulfillment on the New Earth, not in the present Heaven. God's children are destined for life as resurrected beings on a resurrected Earth."[1]

I like the way Dr. Robert Jeffress compared the present and future Heaven.

"Suppose you are about to retire. You decide to purchase land and build a house close to where your grandchildren are living. While you build your house, you live in an apartment temporarily until the house is finished. The apartment is really nice, and you're with your family, but it's not your permanent home." Dr. Jeffress said, "The same thing is true for Christians when we die. When we die right now, we go into the presence of God. We are aware we are with our loved ones, but it is a temporary place. God is building a permanent home for us."[2]

The Bible speaks of Heaven in three different realms.

The First Heaven is the atmosphere. Isaiah describes the first Heaven:

> For just as the heavens are higher than the earth, so my ways are higher than your ways and my thoughts higher than your thoughts. The rain and snow come down from the heavens and stay on the ground to water the earth. They cause the grain to grow, producing seed for the farmer and bread for

the hungry. (Isaiah 55:9,10)

This Heaven describes the sky, the atmosphere above us. There are four spheres: the troposphere (where planes fly through clouds), the stratosphere (where we send weather balloons), the mesosphere (where meteors burn out), and the thermosphere (where a realm of meteors, auroras, and satellites skim through the thermosphere as they circle Earth). The thermosphere marks the edge of space and is the planet's first line of protection against the sun's rays.

Because of space travel, we have been able to fly into this atmosphere with the astronauts and see our beautiful blue marble. On Christmas Eve, December 24, 1968, the crew of Apollo 8 read from the Book of Genesis as they orbited the Moon. Astronauts Bill Anders, Jim Lovell, and Frank Borman, the first humans to travel to the Moon, recited verses 1 through 10 of the Genesis creation narrative from the King James Bible.

> In the beginning, God created the Heaven and the earth. And the earth was without form and void, and darkness was upon the face of the deep. And the Spirit of God moved upon the face of the waters. And God said, 'Let there be light:' and there was light. And God saw the light, that it was good: and God divided the light from the darkness. And God called the light Day, and the darkness he called Night. And the evening and the morning were the first day.
>
> And God said, "Let there be a firmament in the midst of the waters, and let it divide the waters from the waters." And God made the firmament, and divided the waters which were under the firmament from the waters which were above the firmament: and it was so. And God called the firmament Heaven. And the evening and the morning were the second day. (Genesis 1:1-10, King James Version)

Who could have even imagined?

Sore Puzzler or *(I'm So Confused)*

The Second Heaven includes the stars, planets, suns, and galaxies.

> The heavens proclaim the glory of God.
> The skies display his craftsmanship.
> Day after day, they continue to speak;
> night after night they make him known.
> They speak without a sound or word;
> their voice is never heard.
> Yet their Message has gone throughout the earth,
> and their words to all the world.
> God has made a home in the heavens for the sun.
> It bursts forth like a radiant bridegroom after his wedding.
> It rejoices like a great athlete eager to run the race.
> The sun rises at one end of the heavens
> and follows its course to the other end.
> Nothing can hide from its heat. (Psalm 19:1-6)

The Third Heaven is where God dwells. Moses described this Heaven:

> Look, the highest heavens and the earth and everything in it all belong to the Lord your God. (Deuteronomy 10:14)

Jesus prays, "Our Father in *heaven*." (Matthew 6:9)

David writes: The Lord has made the heavens his throne; from there he rules over everything. (Psalm 103:19)

Someday Jerusalem, the Holy City, will come down from this Heaven to become the new Jerusalem:

> And I saw the holy city, the new Jerusalem, coming down from God out of heaven like a bride beautifully dressed for her husband. (Revelation 21:2)

Paul shares with us, the best he can, his experience in the third Heaven:

> I will reluctantly tell about visions and revelations from the Lord. I was caught up to the third Heaven fourteen years ago. Whether I was in my body or out of my body, I don't know—only God knows. Yes, only God knows whether I was in my body or outside my body. But I do know that I was caught up to paradise and heard things so astounding that they cannot be expressed in words, things no human is allowed to tell. (2 Corinthians 12:1-4)

> *Was Paul concerned that people would think that he was making all this up?*

I love how he says he will reluctantly talk about this vision. Did he think people would think he was crazy or just making things up? Did he not have the words to describe this revelation to give it justice? In verse 6, the Message Bible continues:

> "If I had a mind to brag a little, I could probably do it without looking ridiculous, and I'd still be speaking plain truth all the way. But I'll spare you. I don't want anyone imagining me as anything other than the fool you'd encounter if you saw me on the street or heard me talk."

Paul told us he was just an ordinary guy with an extraordinary experience.

Oh my! I'm getting ahead of myself. Let's go back to "What happens the moment we die?" We know there is a third heaven, a spiritual heaven where Jesus ascended to in his physical body. It wasn't like in the movies where people see a ghost streaming out of its body. No, this was no apparition. His disciples stood there on the Mount of Olives, with their mouths open, and witnessed him defy gravity by floating up through the first Heaven or atmosphere until they could no longer see him. Did he float up

Sore Puzzler or *(I'm So Confused)*

through the second Heaven? We don't know that. All we know is that two angels, yes real, white-robed angels, appeared.

> After saying this, he was taken up into a cloud while they were watching, and they could no longer see him. As they strained to see him rising into Heaven, two white-robed men suddenly stood among them. "Men of Galilee," they said, "why are you standing here staring into Heaven? Jesus has been taken from you into Heaven, but someday he will return from Heaven in the same way you saw him go!" (Acts 1:9-11)

> This was no apparition.

Jesus ascended into the third Heaven. Do we follow him after we die?

I was watching a cute video on Instagram the other day. A pastor baptized a little eight-year-old girl. After dunking the child, the conversation went something like this:

Pastor: "So, Sarah, you have been baptized in the name of Jesus. Where are you going now?"

Sarah: "I'm going to Disney World!"

The pastor just laughed.

Our body may be "asleep" after death, but our soul and spirit soar immediately into the present Heaven. Paul experienced this when God took him into the third Heaven. Don't you know, he longed to return to that marvelous place? He said: "I'm torn between two desires: I long to go and be with Christ, which would be far better for me. But for your sake, it is better that I continue to live" (Philippians 1:23).

Do we have a physical body right after death? The simple answer is no. "For then the dust will return to the earth, and the spirit will return to God who gave it" (Ecclesiastics 12:7). Even though Jesus had a physical body, we won't—at least not yet. We can be confident, however, that somehow, someway, we will be with the Lord.

So, we are always confident, even though we know that as

long as we live in these bodies, we are not at home with the Lord. For we live by believing and not by seeing. Yes, we are fully confident, and we would rather be away from these earthly bodies, for then we will be at home with the Lord. (2 Corinthians 5:6-8)

We have all read about NDEs (Near Death Experiences). In 1978, my daddy was dying from cancer. Other than a grandparent, I had never experienced the death of a loved one. Someone told me about Raymond A. Moody's book, *Life After Life*.[3] Dr. Moody interviewed hundreds of men and women who had gone through what was then known as "clinical death." This book and its sequel, *Reflections on Life After Life*,[4] have become a classic. And now, 45 years later, medicine has progressed exponentially, with many people sharing such stories. We must, however, test these stories from a biblical standpoint. These people told stories of while "dying," floating over their bodies and observing their resuscitation. But are their stories different from Paul's journey to the Third Heaven? Some theologians believe that Paul had his NDE when he was stoned and left for dead.

In his blog post, *Another Way In: "Near-Death Experiences" as an Apologetic*, Michael Zigarelli references Norma Bowe, a professor at Kean University. She has recounted this story many times:

"A woman was pronounced dead on arrival at the hospital, but the medical team restored her heartbeat. She later awoke from her coma claiming to have floated over her body while the staff revived her. Nurse Norma Bowe had heard it many times before, dismissing such stories as dreams, brain malfunctions, or drug reactions.

This patient, though, had a habit of memorizing numbers because of her obsessive-compulsive disorder. She told Norma the 12-digit serial number she saw atop the respirator during her out-of-body experience. Norma indulged her, writing it down.

The machine was seven feet high, requiring a maintenance

guy and a ladder to check it out. Yes, there was a number up there, he said. Can you read it to us? Sure, 12 digits—the *exact* number the patient had given to Norma."[5]

Mr. Zigarelli continues:

"For some audiences, it will be a better way into the topic. That's because these kinds of NDEs shift the debate about the supernatural onto the data-driver ground of rationality and reason. In other words, equipped with evidential NDE stories, Christians can step to the naturalist's side of the debate, addressing the big, metaphysical questions *on empirical terms,* not just "religious" terms. So like Paul at Mars Hill (Acts 17), engaging the Greeks from within their worldview, NDE data empowers followers of Jesus to evangelize from within the scientific worldview of their audience. That at least keeps people listening, a prerequisite for persuasion."[6]

I'm still puzzled.

God has many ways for us to reach people and start conversations, doesn't he? What better time to witness to people about the resurrection than when they or a loved one are nearing death?

I'm still puzzled about this intermediate Heaven. What exactly does Paul mean when he says, "Yes, we are fully confident, and we would rather be away from these earthly bodies, for then we will be at home with the Lord" (2 Corinthians 5:8)?

Light-seeds

To be honest, have there been times when you thought heaven was too good to be true? Pie in the sky? Wishful thinking?

What's the difference between the Present (Intermediate) and the Future Heaven?

Describe Paul's vision of the Third Heaven. How does that give you hope?

Our bodies may be asleep after death—but our soul and spirit soar immediately into the Present Heaven. Paul said that he longed to go back there. How is his experience a comfort to you?

Do you know someone who has experienced a Near Death Experience (NDE)? How do you test this through scriptures?

Home

"The Bible takes the word *home* with all its tender associations and sacred memories and applies it to the hereafter and tells us that Heaven is home."[1]

–Author Billy Graham.

10

Yearning To Be at Home With the Lord

In the early 1920s, a young Russian woman named Lillian Ailing was sent by her family from Eastern Europe to see if she could find a safe refuge for them in America. She worked in New York for a time, hoping to save enough money to send to her family so they might join her. She became desperately homesick. She hated New York. After hearing that her family may have been arrested and may be in Siberia, she knew that she had to get home. Realizing she did not have enough money to purchase passage on a steamship, she decided to walk there. Lillian began researching maps and books at the New York Library. In the spring of 1927, this 100-pound, poorly dressed, and pitifully shod young woman started her journey of 6,000 miles. When asked about her destination, she said, "I go to Siberia." Along the way, people tried to dissuade her, even arresting her once in Vancouver for vagrancy to keep her safe long enough to get her through a cold and dangerous winter. She served her sentence and worked in a restaurant until the snow melted when she began her journey again. She reached Dawson City in the Yukon in October 1928, a folk hero by this time.

Walk Me Into Heaven

The Whitehorse Daily Star followed her journey.

"At break-up in the spring of 1929, Lillian Ailing was seen loading her flimsy craft with provisions and a blanket roll and setting off down the mighty Yukon River into the barren vastness of the Arctic. She still had a 2,600-kilometer journey to the Bering Sea.

According to the records, she reached the mouth of the river, left her boat on the beach, and trudged overland toward Bering Strait. Months later, an Eskimo reported seeing a woman beyond Teller, a coastal point near where Alaska and Siberia are closest. She was pulling a small, two-wheel cart."[1]

Did she make it?

In 1972, author Francis Dickie published an account of Alling's journey in *True West* magazine.[2] Shortly after that article was written, a reader named Arthur Elmore wrote to Mr. Dickie, recalling a strange story told by a Russian friend. In the fall of 1930, Elmore's friend was on the waterfront of Provideniya, Russia, 150 miles west of Nome. On the beach were several officials interrogating a group—three Eskimo men and one Caucasian woman, standing near a boat. It is uncertain whether this woman was, in fact, Lillian Ailing.[3]

Lillian was desperate to get home. There was no stopping her; the longing was too great.

If you love Jesus, there's a yearning in you, also, to be *at home* with him.

> Therefore, we are always confident and know that as long as we are at home in the body, we are away from the Lord. (2 Corinthians 5:6, NIV)

I know what that yearning is to the at home with the Lord. I will never forget that day. It was the summer of 1981. My mother-in-law called me over to her house. "We have something to tell you." Curious, I walked into her living room. My mother and mother-in-law sat on the couch, drinking coffee. They were both smiling from ear to ear.

"Yes?" I smiled back at them.

"We want to take you to Israel!"

"Israel?" Stunned, I did not know what to say.

On October 2, 1981, twelve of us boarded the plane toward the Holy Land. Truly a dream come true. I wrote this in my journal as we prepared for our landing in Tel Aviv.

> "We arrived at Tel Aviv after a hilarious plane ride. There was an air of excitement around the plane. The people were constantly up and around, milling all over the cabin. The steward tried to get everyone to sit down and prepare for landing, but people kept popping up here and there. One lady absolutely refused to sit down, so the stewardess (that's what they were called back in the day) just threw her hands up, said something in Hebrew, sat down in her jump seat, and buckled up. When we landed, people were jumping all over one another to get off the plane. Several of them bent down and kissed the ground. They were finally home."

The trip was beautiful. We traveled from Galilee down to the Red Sea. When I returned home to Arkansas, I felt a restlessness or disquiet that I couldn't quite understand. I was home with my family, and life went on, but it was as if I felt homesick and not where I truly belonged. Forty-two years later, I can still recall those feelings.

In the Intermediate Heaven, we will be at home with the Lord. Our physical body will be "asleep," but our spirit and soul, the essence of our being, will be with Jesus.

Paul said God placed this longing in us to live with him forever; it's in our DNA. It's not

> **God placed a longing within us to live with him forever.**

that we want to leave our families anytime soon and go to Heaven; it's that if we live in these bodies, we are not truly home. There's nothing psychologically wrong with that. It's the way God created us.

Men and women throughout history have tried to meet that longing in different ways. They seek after riches but don't find him. They drink alcohol or take drugs but don't find him. They marry the love of their life and have children but don't find him. They take enormous risks like skydiving or mountain climbing but don't find him. They travel the world or buy beautiful mansions but don't find him. God isn't hiding out in some heavenly place; he's right here in plain sight. Only God can fill that hole, meet that need, or give us true happiness. This world is not our home.

> God isn't hiding out in some heavenly place.

> For we know that if the earthly tent we live in is destroyed, we have a building from God, an eternal house in Heaven, not built by human hands. Meanwhile, we groan, longing to be clothed instead with our heavenly dwelling, because when we are clothed, we will not be found naked. For while we are in this tent, we groan and are burdened, because we do not wish to be unclothed but to be clothed instead with our heavenly dwelling, so that what is mortal may be swallowed up by life. (2 Corinthians 5:1-4, NIV)

We long to be clothed in that heavenly dwelling. What kind of body will we have in the intermediate or present Heaven?

> We grow weary in our present bodies, and we long to put on our heavenly bodies like new clothing. (2 Corinthians 5:2)

Randy Alcorn writes:
"A fundamental article of the Christian faith is that the resurrected Christ now dwells in Heaven. We are told that his resurrected body on Earth was physical and that this same, physical Jesus ascended to Heaven, from where He will one day return to Earth. It seems indisputable, then, to say that there is at least one phys-

ical body in the present Heaven. If Christ's body in the intermediate Heaven has physical properties, it stands to reason that others in Heaven could have physical forms as well, even if only temporary ones.

To avoid misunderstanding, I need to emphasize a critical doctrinal point. According to scripture, we do *not* receive resurrection bodies immediately after death. Resurrection does not happen one at a time. *If* we have intermediate forms in the intermediate Heaven, they will not be our true bodies, which we leave behind at death."[4]

Think of the Transfiguration. Jesus took his three closest disciples up on the mountain for the experience of their lives.

> Six days later, three of them saw that glory. Jesus took Peter and the brothers, James and John, and led them up a high mountain. His appearance changed from the inside out, right before their eyes. Sunlight poured from his face. His clothes were filled with light.

Oh wow. Jesus was "transfigured." The word "transfiguration" comes from the Latin roots trans ("across") and figura ("form, shape"). It signifies a change of form or appearance. These men had never seen the light like this. Jesus illuminated. They could only compare the shining to the sun's brightness; they didn't know about lasers or electricity. I can't even imagine. And then there were three.

> Then they realized that Moses and Elijah were also there in deep conversation with him. (Matthew 17:1-3, Message)

Then they realized . . . At first, they did not see the other two people. Perhaps the dazzling light blinded them. But there they were—two men dead for centuries in bodily form. Moses was the giver of the law, and Elijah was the prophet. Jesus was the fulfillment of both. I often wondered how the disciples knew who they were. Did Jesus introduce them? How would they have known unless Jesus told them?

As Stephen, the martyr, fell to the ground, broken and bleeding from the stones, he looked up into the Intermediate Heaven and saw Jesus standing beside the right hand of God.

> But Stephen, full of the Holy Spirit, gazed steadily into Heaven and saw the glory of God, and he saw Jesus standing in the place of honor at God's right hand. And he told them, "Look, I see the heavens opened and the Son of Man standing in the place of honor at God's right hand. (Acts 7:55-56)

Wayne Grudem points out that Stephen "did not see mere symbols of a state of existence. It was rather that his eyes were opened to see a spiritual dimension of reality that God has hidden from us in this present age, a dimension which nonetheless really does exist in our space/time universe, and within which Jesus now lives in his physical resurrected body, waiting even now for a time when he will return to earth."[5]

God allowed Elijah's servant to see into Heaven—see angels. Remember the story. The king of Aram was at war with Israel. Every time he planned a maneuver, God told Elijah, and he let the king of Israel know. Angry, the king of Aram sent an army to surround the city and capture Elijah. One morning when Elijah's servant went out, he saw the army. Frightened, he went back in to tell Elijah.

> "Don't be afraid," the prophet answered. "Those who are with us are more than those who are with them."
> And Elisha prayed, "Open his eyes, Lord, so that he may see." Then the Lord opened the servant's eyes, and he looked and saw the hills full of horses and chariots of fire all around Elisha. (2 Kings 6:16,17, NIV)

Yes, the Heaven we long for is more authentic than the world we live in now.

No matter what, we are with Jesus in the Intermediate Heaven.

Yearning To Be at Home With the Lord

Paul was "convinced." Nothing could dissuade him.

> For I am convinced [and continue to be convinced—beyond any doubt] that neither death, nor life, nor angels, nor principalities, nor things present *and* threatening, nor things to come, nor powers, nor height, nor depth, nor any other created thing, will be able to separate us from the [unlimited] love of God, which is in Christ Jesus our Lord. (Romans 8:38, 39, Amplified)

> The Heaven we long for is more authentic than the world we live in now.

We also know that the Holy Spirit is in us.

> "The Spirit of God, who raised Jesus from the dead, lives in you. And just as God raised Christ Jesus from the dead, he will give life to your mortal bodies by this same Spirit living within you." (Romans 8:11)

How long will we stay in the intermediate state or intermediate Heaven? We read in Revelation 6 about "the souls of those killed because they had held firm in their witness to the Word of God." They gathered under the Altar and cried out to God for judgment against their killers, but they were given a white robe and told to sit back and wait.

I don't have much patience here in my earthly life. But as our spirit and soul unite with Jesus in the intermediate Heaven, waiting will not be difficult.

But boy, oh boy! What awaits us when the trumpet sounds and Jesus gathers those from Heaven and comes down to Earth? Now, the fun part begins.

"Then after a Honeymoon in Heaven, Christ will come to reign on the earth." John Rice[6]

Light-seeds

Therefore, we are always confident and know that as long as we are at home in the body, we are away from the Lord (2 Corinthians 5:6). How does this scripture give you confidence?

How do people you know try to find peace—or fill that God-given longing for him?

Does the Transfiguration confirm life after death to you?

Occasionally, God peels back this earthly dimension (like Elijah's servant seeing the angel army). Does that confirm the authenticity of a different world than we live in now?

Paul was convinced nothing could separate him from God. Are you?

11

"Look, I Am Making All Things New"
(A Fresh Start)

"It will be as if an artist wiped away the old paint,
stained and cracking, and started a new
and better painting, but using the same images
on the same canvas."

—Randy Acorn[1]

Everyone loves a fresh start—back to square one—a clean sweep. God is no exception. He is all about new starts. In the beginning, God created Heaven and earth and declared them good. Yes, very good. God made a place of breathtaking beauty. Exquisite. Perfection. He placed Adam and Eve in this paradise with only one job: to oversee and enjoy his creation. We know the rest of the story. Sin entered this wonderland, and the earth was never the same again.

Anthony Hoekema wrote:
"Because of man's fall into sin, a curse was pronounced over the creation. God now sent His Son into this world to redeem that creation from the results of sin. The

work of Christ, therefore, is not just to save certain individuals, not even to save an innumerable throng of blood-bought people. The complete work of Christ is nothing less than to redeem the entire creation from the effects of sin. That purpose will not be accomplished until God has ushered in the new earth until Paradise Lost becomes Paradise Regained."[2]

God so loved the world (*kosmos– the entire created order*) that He sent His Son. (John 3:16)

Yes, God had a plan for the entire created order. Someday, somehow, he would begin again. But first, God had to start by dealing with sin. If he were to create a new earth, it had to be filled with recreated people. How was he going to do that? We know the rest of the story. He sent Jesus to the old, sinful earth to take care of sin once and for all. Jesus completed his assignment and went back to Heaven to wait—wait with those who have been waiting with him in the present Heaven—wait for the trumpet sound. Holy goosebumps!

> If God creates a new earth, it has to be filled with recreated people.

But let me reveal to you a wonderful secret. We will not all die, but we will all be transformed! It will happen in a moment, in the blink of an eye, when the last trumpet is blown. For when the trumpet sounds, those who have died will be raised to live forever. And we who are living will also be transformed. For our dying bodies must be transformed into bodies that will never die; our mortal bodies must be transformed into immortal bodies. (1 Corinthians 15:51-53)

People today are all about saving the earth. It has become a religion to some. Yes, we need to care for God's handiwork, but not to the point of worshipping that creation. The Bible tells us that this earth will someday be renewed, not by us, but by God.

"Look, I Am Making All Things New" *(A Fresh Start)*

He is the only one who can do that. At this point, he is more interested in recreating his people than his earth.

Our old earth is slowly deteriorating, groaning. Paul writes:

> For all creation is waiting eagerly for that future day when God will reveal who his children really are. Against its will, all creation was subjected to God's curse. But with eager hope, the creation looks forward to the day when it will join God's children in glorious freedom from death and decay. For we know that all creation has been groaning as in the pains of childbirth right up to the present time. (Romans 8:18-22)

God promises that someday he will make all things fresh and new (Revelation 21:5). This is not unique to the New Testament. God proclaimed early on that this was his plan.

> Look! I am creating new heavens and a new earth, and no one will even think about the old ones anymore. Be glad; rejoice forever in my creation. (Isaiah 65:17, 18)

> "As surely as my new heavens and earth will remain, so will you always be my people, with a name that will never disappear," says the Lord. (Isaiah 66:22)

At the end of his life, the Romans arrested the apostle John and banished him to the island of Patmos. He probably thought his usefulness for God was over, but God gave him a vision, a revelation, that placed hope in all of us more than 2,000 years later.

> This is a revelation from Jesus Christ, which God gave him to show his servants the events that must soon take place. He sent an angel to present this revelation to his servant John, who faithfully reported everything he saw. This is his report of the word of God and the testimony of Jesus Christ. (Revelation 1:1, 2)

Walk Me Into Heaven

God sent an angel to show John unimaginable things. I can picture him waking up each morning and quickly sitting at his desk and writing down everything he had heard and seen. The first part of the revelation was terrifying and probably as confusing to John as it is to us, but he faithfully recorded it. And then. Oh, my goodness. What he saw—to describe it as well as he did even now, 2,000 years later. What a vision!

> Then I saw a new heaven and a new earth, for the old heaven and the old earth had disappeared. And the sea was also gone. And I saw the holy city, the new Jerusalem, coming down from God out of heaven like a bride beautifully dressed for her husband.
>
> **John saw a New Heaven and a New Earth.**
>
> I heard a loud shout from the throne, saying, "Look, God's home is now among his people! He will live with them, and they will be his people. God himself will be with them. He will wipe every tear from their eyes, and there will be no more death or sorrow or crying or pain. All these things are gone forever."
>
> And the one sitting on the throne said, "Look, I am making everything new!" And then he said to me, "Write this down, for what I tell you is trustworthy and true." And he also said, "It is finished! I am the Alpha and the Omega—the Beginning and the End. To all who are thirsty, I will give freely from the springs of the water of life. All who are victorious will inherit all these blessings, and I will be their God, and they will be my children." (Revelation 21:1-7)

Peter looked forward to this new heaven and new earth.

> But we are looking forward to the new heavens and new earth he has promised, a world filled with God's righteousness. (2 Peter 3:13)

"Look, I Am Making All Things New" *(A Fresh Start)*

Will the old earth be destroyed, or will it be renewed? (Think of all the renovation shows on HGTV these days.) Theologians differ from each other. Those who believe in complete obliteration quote scriptures like this:

> Since everything around us is going to be destroyed like this, what holy and godly lives you should live, looking forward to the day of God and hurrying it along. On that day, he will set the heavens on fire, and the elements will melt away in the flames. (2 Peter 3:11, 12)

> Then I saw a new heaven and a new earth, for the old heaven and the old earth had disappeared. And the sea was also gone. (Revelations 21:1)

Let's put on our theologian hat and dig deeper into the Greek. (Not too deep, I promise.) In his blog, *Life, Hope, and Truth,* Paul Luecke explains 2 Peter 3:13: "But we are looking forward to the new heavens and the new earth he has promised, a world filled with God's righteousness."

"The Greek word Peter uses in 2 Peter 3:13 for "new" is *kainos*, which refers to a state of freshness (something that is qualitatively new or renewed), rather than the Greek word *neos*, which means new in terms of age. Whether the earth is entirely consumed by this fire, or the surface is melted and thereby purified, the end result will still be a planet that is "new"—remade or refashioned by God. We see that it is still called the "earth"

> *Kainos*—A state of freshness.

and that the heavens will likewise be made "new."[3]

Brandon Andress concurs with the new and restored earth theory. "Interestingly enough, it is the word *kainos* that Paul uses to describe the Christian, as a new (*kainos*) creation. The individual Christian has not been vaporized into non-existence and newly created, rather the old (*archaios*) has passed away, and the new (*kainos*) has come."[4] Those who belong to Christ are new (*kainos*) people.

The old life is gone; a new life has begun! (2 Corinthians 5:17)

God is the Alpha and Omega, the beginning and the end. Isn't it interesting that the end in Revelation mirrors the beginning in Genesis? Even the word "resurrection" depicts a new life that ends and a new life that begins.

Gregory Stevenson writes:

> "In his resurrection, Christ defeated death not only for humanity but for creation as well. Just as the death of Christ's body affected the resurrection of that body as a new creation no longer subject to suffering and decay, the passing away of the first heaven and the first earth leads to a new heaven and a new earth which is no longer subject to death or pain. As the story of Christ is incomplete without the resurrection, so too is the story of creation incomplete without resurrection. Again, the emphasis here is on continuity. God's new creation is the completion and fulfillment of the old creation (the goal) just as our resurrected bodies are the ultimate goal for our bodies. The end goal (telos) of this story is that God makes all things new."[5]

What will this new earth be like? Will it be a recreated and restored garden of Eden? Think about when you held perfection in your hands: a newborn baby, a tiny puppy (think puppy breath!), a rosebud. Imagine the most beautiful sunset that you have ever seen, walking on a glistening white beach along a turquoise ocean or climbing to the top of a mountain for a 360-degree view of the robin egg blue sky above and the emerald green valley below. Just picture walking among thousands of brilliantly colored hummingbirds. I love fresh, natural fragrances like citrus, evergreen, lavender, sage, basil, and rosemary. All summer long,

"Look, I Am Making All Things New" *(A Fresh Start)*

I enjoy their sweet, woodsy scents. As I'm writing this, it's winter. Yesterday, I pulled up the dead stems of a lavender plant. This spring, I will replace those plants with new, healthy ones. The new earth will be like that. No putrid odors—decay, deterioration, or death will exist on the new earth.

> The LORD will comfort Israel again. Her desert will blossom like Eden, her barren wilderness like the garden of the LORD. Joy and gladness will be found there. Songs of thanksgiving will fill the air. (Isaiah 51:3)

> But with eager hope, the creation looks forward to the day when it will join God's children in glorious freedom from death and decay. (Romans 8:21)

The new earth will be the earth today at its best. It won't be some unrecognizable, futuristic, *"Star Warian"* (is that a word?) kind of place. It will be familiar yet fresh and new, an eternity of delightful and pleasing surprises. Some think the new earth will be even better than the Garden of Eden. The first garden was beautiful, but we know there was potential for evil to mar its perfection. The new earth will have none of that because Jesus settled that once and for all. We will be safe and secure knowing that evil has been banished. True "shalom."

Light-seeds

Anthony Hoekema wrote that the *complete* work of Christ is nothing less than to redeem the entire creation from the effects of sin. The *entire* creation? God is the only one who can save ALL of his creation. Paul says all creation is groaning. Have you thought about that in those terms?

Will the old earth be destroyed, or will it be renewed? What are your thoughts on the Greek word "kainos," or a state of freshness as Paul describes in 2 Peter 3:13 and the "new" Christian in 2 Corinthians 5:17?

Gregory Stevenson wrote: "In his resurrection, Christ defeated death not only for humanity but for creation as well." How does that encourage you?

How do you picture perfection on the New Earth?

12

Spending Forever Time With Jesus
or *(The Best Part)*

"It's not about the destination; it's Him."
Pastor Derek Smith, 2023

"As Jesus and the disciples continued on their way to Jerusalem, they came to a certain village where a woman named Martha welcomed him into her home. Her sister, Mary, sat at the Lord's feet, listening to what he taught." (Luke 10:38, 39)

The early morning is my favorite time of day. I have always been an early riser. I love the quiet of the morning. I usually wake up at about 4:45, grab that first cup of coffee, my Bible, my computer, and spend the next two hours with Jesus. That's when I pray, read his word, and write. I've often sat in my chair and wondered, what will it be like in Heaven? How will we spend time with the Lord? How does that even work? The only thing we have to go by now is the scriptures that point to that forever relationship with him. Why would it be any different in Heaven?

Several years ago, I wrote a book of stories based on different people in the New Testament (*To See Him Face to Face*).[1] I wrote these stories in the first person, using words directly from scripture. They took me into the lives of ordinary men and women during the time of Jesus. My favorite part of writing each story would be when the character looked at the face of Jesus. Here is an excerpt from the story of the woman with the issue of blood. She had just reached through the crowd and touched the fringe (*tzitzit*) on the hem of his prayer shawl (*tallit*).

> "In a daze, I heard Jesus say, 'Who touched me' (Luke 8:45)? The disciple beside him said, 'Master, the people are crowding and pressing against you.'
>
> Jesus began looking around. 'No, someone touched me; I know that power has gone out from me' (Luke 8:46 NIV).
>
> Jesus continued to look over the crowd until his eyes met mine. Those piercing eyes looked into my very soul. Trembling but no longer feeling any shame, I fell to my knees in front of Jesus. My story began to pour out of me. Gently, he helped me to my feet. His eyes never left my face. Finally, he said tenderly, 'Daughter, your faith has healed you. Go in peace.'" (Luke 8:48 NIV)

"His eyes never left her face." Can't you put yourself there? Even though there was a crowd of people pressing into him, Jesus could single out that one precious soul and give her his undivided attention. That will be the way it is in Heaven. God is omnipresent. He can be everywhere at one time. How in the world does that work? It's easier in today's technological age to believe this. Millions of people can interrelate on the internet at one time. God's capacity to interact with his people goes way beyond that. It exceeds anything that we can even imagine. Revelation 1:7 tells us that "every eye will see him." And in 1 John 3:2: "Dear friends, we are already God's children, but he has not yet shown us what we will be like when Christ appears. But we do know that we will be like him, for we will see him as he really is."

God created us to have fellowship with him. Revelation 3:20 reads:

> Look! I stand at the door and knock. If you hear my voice and open the door, I will come in, and we will share a meal together as friends. Those who are victorious will sit with me on my throne, just as I was victorious and sat with my Father on his throne. (Revelation 3:20, 21)

> There are many examples in the Bible about God desiring friendship with us.

Jesus was not some divine man or Wizard of Oz who hid behind a curtain and placed himself in a holy sanctuary beyond the reach of ordinary people. He was one of us. He was also a God who got down and dirty with his followers, experiencing everything they experienced. It was all about having a relationship with them.

In the Garden of Eden, Adam and Eve sadly hid from God when they heard him walking in the cool of the evening. They had just eaten the forbidden fruit. The scripture leads me to think that God took a stroll with them each evening in the cool of the day, so they hid, knowing he was coming. Can you imagine strolling with Jesus in the cool of the day? How sad that their time with him was cut short because of sin, but God was determined to restore that relationship with his children.

Over and over in the scriptures, we read of God reaching out to his people, sometimes through dreams, angels, and sometimes in person. There are eight recorded appearances in the Bible where God took on a physical form: He appeared to Hagar (Genesis 16:13), Abraham and Sarah at Mamre (Genesis 18:1-33), Abraham on Mount Moriah (Genesis 22:11-14), Jacob at Peniel (Genesis 32:24-32), Moses in the Burning Bush (Exodus 3:2-4:17), Gideon (Judges 6:11-24), Samson's parents (Judges 13:2-23), and with the three men in the fiery furnace (Daniel 3:23-29). God was not a stranger. These incidences foreshadow God coming to earth, the incarnation—the man, Jesus, the Christ. Job tells us that we will see God. "I will see him for myself. Yes, I will see him with my own eyes (Job 19:27).

In the New Testament, Jesus walked among the people, teaching, healing the sick, performing miracles, and raising the dead. But the most important act of God on earth was to demonstrate to us how much he loved us by spending time with his people—showing us through Jesus what our relationship with him would be like throughout eternity.

Jesus loved a party. Can you imagine him with his disciples at the wedding in Cana? They were eating, drinking, and dancing, having so much fun. He cared enough for the bride and groom's families that he replenished the wine to avoid embarrassment and saved them from a social disaster. Jesus showed that he loved everyone, from the rich to the poor. He cared if they were sick or hurt. He had

> Jesus loved a party.

meaningful conversations with women. Think of the woman at the well, Mary Magdalene, or Mary and Martha. He didn't care that society gave little thought to women or their ideas at the time. He had intellectual conversations with everyone from Pharisees and Sadducees to tax collectors and sinners. The New Testament is a testament to Jesus, the Son of Man, who interacted daily with people—foreshadowing Heaven.

In my book, *To See Him Face to Face,* I often portray conversations with Jesus. Here is one between Jesus and John on the mountain right before the Transfiguration.

> "We watched the sun sink into the horizon, sending out waves of exquisite light and bathing the valley in pink, brown, green, and blue hues. The evening settled over us. I was restless, getting up often to stretch my legs. Jesus beckoned me to sit by him on the edge of the bluff. Sitting beside him and talking gave me peace, calming my restless spirit. We talked of home and our mothers and families. He told me a little about what to expect in

the coming weeks. I shared with him my worries and fears. Talking to Jesus was always so easy. He listened with his eyes as well as his ears. I never sensed that he was bored or tired of my chatter."[2]

Eternity will be like that. Imagine having deep and intimate one-on-one conversations with Jesus whenever we want. Many questions have bothered me over the years. Having a face-to-face with Jesus will be so good. I have my list ready to go!

Jesus appreciated a good meal. So much happened during the meals Jesus shared with his disciples, tax collectors, and even sinners. He used these times to fellowship, teach, and have good conversations. Relationships were important to him. How much more will we sit around the table with Jesus in Heaven? Think of the meal Jesus shared with the disciples on the beach of the Sea of Galilee after his resurrection. He brought his friends together, fed them, and spent time with them. Yes, we will have many delicious meals with Jesus—even feasts! Jesus talks about this feast in Matthew 8:11. He had just healed a soldier's friend. Praising the man's faith, he told his disciples: "This man is the vanguard of many outsiders who will soon be coming from all directions—streaming in from the east, pouring in from the west, sitting down at God's kingdom banquet alongside Abraham, Isaac, and Jacob." We'll get to sit at the table with the great heroes of the faith, men and women who have gone before us. Imagine the stories that they will tell!

> Imagine sitting around the table with Jesus.

> Let us be glad and rejoice and let us give honor to him. For the time has come for the wedding feast of the Lamb, and his bride has prepared herself. She has been given the finest of pure white linen to wear. For the fine linen represents the good deeds of God's holy people. And the angel said to me, "Write this: Blessed are those who are invited to the wedding feast of the Lamb." And he added, "These are true words that come from God." (Revelation 19:7-9)

Isaiah had already spoken of this remarkable feast:

> In Jerusalem, the Lord of Heaven's Armies
> will spread a wonderful feast
> for all the people of the world.
> It will be a delicious banquet
> with clear, well-aged wine and choice meat.
> There he will remove the cloud of gloom,
> the shadow of death that hangs over the earth.
> He will swallow up death forever!
> The Sovereign Lord will wipe away all tears.
> He will remove forever all insults and mockery
> against his land and people. (Isaiah 25:6-8)

We will feast with Jesus and be clothed in pure white linen—even after Labor Day! (Only those of my generation understand that rule.) My spiritual mother, Ruth, always looked forward to this Marriage Supper, eating whatever she wanted without worrying about calories.

Scripture repeatedly points out what God has planned for us in Heaven with him. We will "worship the Lord with gladness." Authentic worship will be an essential part of our heavenly life, but not all of it. Some people believe that eternity consists of only one long church service. Has church become tantamount to boredom? That's a sad commentary on our churches today—or on us. No, worship in Heaven will be beautiful and pure, filling our spirits so that we almost burst with joy! All focus will be on God.

> *Authentic worship will be an essential part of our heavenly life.*

There will be no sin that corrupts our adulation. Genuine, sincere, honest praise will flow out of this heavenly worship. The Bible is full of scriptures praising God here on earth. How much more will we praise him in Heaven?

Psalm 100 captures the true worship of El Shaddai:

Spending Forever Time With Jesus or *(The Best Part)*

> Shout with joy to the Lord, all the earth!
> Worship the Lord with gladness.
> Come before him, singing with joy.
> Acknowledge that the Lord is God!
> He made us, and we are his.
> We are his people, the sheep of his pasture.
> Enter his gates with thanksgiving.
> Go into his courts with praise.
> Give thanks to him and praise his name.
> For the Lord is good.
> His unfailing love continues forever,
> and his faithfulness continues to each generation.
> (Psalm 100)

Yesterday in church, we sang the *Revelation Song* by Jennie Le Riddle. When she wrote the song, most worship songs were more about prayer, emphasizing the person praying and not God. There were a lot of "I" and "me" in the songs. But this song was all about praising the Lord God Almighty.

> "Worthy is the Lamb who was slain
> Holy, holy is He
> Sing a new song to Him who sits on
> Heaven's mercy seat."[3]

How often have I been in prayer or a worship service, and my mind wanders, skipping from one thought to another? When we worship God on the New Earth, we will have no trouble focusing our thoughts on him. The love that we feel from God will immerse us in his glory. There will be no room in our brains for anything else but him. We will display pure and humble physical expressions of worship to our Holy God.

Many years ago, I attended a Billy Graham revival at War Memorial Stadium in Little Rock, Arkansas. I don't know how many people were there, but the stadium holds around 54,000. It

Walk Me Into Heaven

was packed, and it was glorious. Standing with that many people and praising God was an experience I would never forget. When we stand together in the very throne room of God, there will be billions—yes, billions of people and angels singing praises to God. How can I wrap my mind around that?

The book of Revelation describes this continuous praise around God's throne.

> And they were singing the song of Moses, the servant of God, and the song of the Lamb:
> "Great and marvelous are your works,
> O Lord God, the Almighty.
> Just and true are your ways,
> O King of the nations.
> Who will not fear you, Lord,
> and glorify your name?
> For you alone are holy." (Revelation 15:3,4)

> And from the throne came a voice that said,
> "Praise our God,
> all his servants,
> all who fear him,
> from the least to the greatest."
> Then I heard again what sounded like the shout of a vast crowd or the roar of mighty ocean waves or the crash of loud thunder:
> "Praise the Lord!
> For the Lord our God, the Almighty reigns.
> Let us be glad and rejoice,
> and let us give honor to him.
> For the time has come for the wedding feast of the Lamb, and his bride has prepared herself.
> She has been given the finest of pure white linen to wear. For the fine linen represents the good deeds of God's holy people." (Revelation 19:5-8)

Spending Forever Time With Jesus or *(The Best Part)*

John MacArthur describes this worship so well:
"Far from being stuffy and uncomfortable, our worship in Heaven will bring us sheer pleasure. It will be unhindered enjoyment of God, unadulterated by any taint of guilt or any fear of insecurity. None of our earthly pleasures can compare with the perfect delight we will derive from heavenly worship. All the joys we derive from earthly love, earthly beauty, and other earthly blessings are nothing in comparison to the pure bliss of heavenly worship before the very face of Him from whom all true blessings flow. Only those who know Him can even begin to appreciate the unadulterated pleasure this will be."[4]

No rock concert or church service can ever compare or come remotely close to this glorious time together in front of the throne. I can't wait to join in with my grandchildren!

Light-seeds

God showed us, through Jesus, what spending one on one time will look like. He created us for that very reason. What does spending one on one time with Jesus look like to you?

Will our one-on-one time with Jesus be only spiritual, or will we also fellowship with him—just for fun?

Authentic worship will be an essential part of our heavenly life. How will it be different in Heaven?

Imagine standing or bowing in the very throne room of God, worshipping with billions of people!

13

The Holy City—The New Jerusalem
or *(City Girl or Country Girl?)*

And look! I will create Jerusalem as a place of happiness.
Her people will be a source of joy.
I will rejoice over Jerusalem
and delight in my people.
And the sound of weeping and crying
will be heard in it no more. (Isaiah 65:18, 19)

I was a city girl raised in Tulsa, Oklahoma, for the first part of my life. It was an idyllic childhood, the best of both worlds. Our house was in the suburbs, but we were only a short distance from downtown. Back then, before colossal shopping centers and Walmart, we'd dress up, get on a city bus and ride downtown to shop. Mother and I would spend the day going to different department stores.

At noon, we often ended up at the lunch counter at Woolworth's for a fountain Coke and a grilled cheese sandwich. Sometimes we'd "dine" in the Tea Room at Vandever's. I always felt so special when we did that. After lunch, we would finish our shopping at Seidenbach's Department Store. I was always a little scared about walking through the revolving door, afraid I would trip. Back then, the cosmetic and perfume department was always the first place you walked through. I still remember the sweet fragrance of perfume and makeup as we entered the store. The shoe department was one of my favorite places because I could try on shoes and then step on this cool X-ray machine and look down to see where my bones fit. Yep, probably not very good for us. I also loved getting on an elevator and watching the pretty attendant turn the lever and take me to the different floors. The only thing I didn't like about elevators was that being very small, I seemed to be always squished to the back when people got on and off.

At the end of the long day, we would catch a bus back home, tired but happy. I couldn't wait to get home and try on my new shoes!

Do I want to be a city girl in New Jerusalem? Fifteen different times, Revelation mentions this is the place where God and his people lived.

> "Everyone knows what a city is—a place with buildings, streets, and residences occupied by people and subject to a common government. Cities have inhabitants, visitors, bustling activity, cultural events, and gatherings involving music, the arts, education, religion, entertainment, and athletics. If the capital city of the New Earth doesn't have these defining characteristics of a city, it would seem misleading for Scripture to repeatedly call it a city." (Randy Alcorn).[1]

Unfortunately, fear, crime, corruption, drugs, homelessness, and filth fill our cities today—so different from the city of my childhood. Thankfully, the New Jerusalem is the antithesis of our present-day municipalities.

For the last 53 years, I have been a country girl living in a small farming community. For the most part, it was a wonderful place to raise our kids. My husband's parents lived next door, and my mother lived down the street. My children enjoyed bike riding, three-wheeler riding at the farm (not too safe), and kids

The Holy City–The New Jerusalem or *(City Girl or Country Girl?)*

going to each other's houses. Everyone knew what everyone else was doing. We looked out for each other. Small-town life was not perfect, however. The enemy still found a way to raise his ugly head even there.

So—on the New Earth, will Heaven be a city? Will Heaven be a country? Will it be both? I think it will. The New Earth will be so breathtakingly beautiful that I can't even begin to try and describe it. We have only God's words: "A bride beautifully dressed!"

> Then I saw a new heaven and a new earth, for the old heaven and the old earth had disappeared. And the sea was also gone. And I saw the holy city, the new Jerusalem, coming down from God out of heaven like a bride beautifully dressed for her husband.
>
> I heard a loud shout from the throne, saying, "Look, God's home is now among his people! He will live with them, and they will be his people. God himself will be with them. He will wipe every tear from their eyes, and there will be no more death or sorrow or crying or pain. All these things are gone forever. (Revelation 21:1-4)

The Holy City!

The Holy City—the New Jerusalem! Did you know that we are already citizens of the New Heaven? We don't live there yet, but someday we will.

> But we are citizens of heaven, where the Lord Jesus Christ lives. And we are eagerly waiting for him to return as our Savior. (Philippians 3:20)

This Holy City—what will it be like? The most important thing: "God's home is with his people." He will live right there with us. It will be a place where there is only joy, happiness, bliss, and delight—how many adjectives can I conjure up in my mind?

There will be no more sorrow or pain or crying or distress. God will wipe away all tears. The Lord's prayer says, "On earth as it is in Heaven." Finally! Heaven will come down, and Earth will be Heaven—perfection.

How does Revelation describe the New Jerusalem? "It shone with the glory of God and sparkled like a precious stone—like jasper as clear as crystal" (Revelation 21:11). Jasper is usually opaque and green, but this stone is as clear as crystal—depicting God's glory.

> The City shimmered like a precious gem, light-filled, pulsing light. She had a wall majestic and high with twelve gates. At each gate stood an Angel, and on the gates were inscribed the names of the Twelve Tribes of the sons of Israel: three gates on the east, three gates on the north, three gates on the south, three gates on the west. The wall was set on twelve foundations, the names of the Twelve Apostles of the Lamb inscribed on them. (Revelation 21:12b-14, Message)

The City shimmered—sparkled or glittered—like fresh snow on a sunny day—clean, dazzling, pulsing light. She (notice that New Jerusalem is a "she") had a wall that was majestic and high with twelve ginormous (is this a word now?) gates.

> The angel who talked to me held in his hand a gold measuring stick to measure the city, its gates, and its wall. (Revelation 21:15)

The angel is carrying a golden ruler or measuring stick. Do we take this literally? John is precise in his description of the New Jerusalem. A good rule to go by when studying the Bible is to take everything literally unless it doesn't make sense to do so. The Bible is very exact at times. In Genesis, the instructions that God gave Noah on how to build the ark are detailed and meticulous. He showed Moses the blueprint before constructing the original Jerusalem Tabernacle and Solomon before he built

The Holy City–The New Jerusalem or *(City Girl or Country Girl?)*

the First Temple. Yes, we can trust the description God gave for the New Jerusalem. Oh, my goodness!

> When he measured it, he found it was a square, as wide as it was long. In fact, its length and width and height were each 1,400 miles. Then he measured the walls and found them to be 216 feet thick (according to the human standard used by the angel). (Revelation 21:16, 17)

Notice that this says it is being measured according to human standards so that we can wrap our finite minds around it. Yes, I believe that the city is "literally" this big. The New Jerusalem is a cube—1,400 miles by 1,400 miles by 1,400 miles. The New Jerusalem will be larger than India, with around 2 million square miles. There will be plenty of room in this city for everyone. The size of the New Jerusalem boggles my mind.

Then God gave John the words to describe the wall of the New Jerusalem.

> The wall was made of jasper, and the city was pure gold, as clear as glass. The wall of the city was built on foundation stones inlaid with twelve precious stones: the first was jasper, the second sapphire, the third agate, the fourth emerald, the fifth onyx, the sixth carnelian, the seventh chrysolite, the eighth beryl, the ninth topaz, the tenth chrysoprase, the eleventh jacinth, the twelfth amethyst. (Revelation 21:18-20)

Why is there a wall around the New Jerusalem?

This breathtakingly beautiful wall was made of jasper and anchored by twelve foundation stones of precious jewels. Twelve symbolizes perfection or eternal completion. The number twelve often comes up in the Bible. Why is there a need for a wall around the city? Perhaps God is telling John that some will be allowed in and some will not. Or it symbolizes that we are finally safe and secure, never having to worry or be fearful again because God cast all enemies of the Kingdom into the lake of fire.

There are twelve gates around the city, three on each side. Inscribed on each gate is an apostle's name. An angel stands guard, letting in only those whose "names are written in the Lamb's Book of Life" (vs. 27). We know that God sent an angel to guard Eden after the fall of man, so why wouldn't God place an angel to protect the new Eden? Revelation 21 tells us that angels are standing at the gates. This sends a message that the city is safe and secure. In ancient times, business and proclamations occurred at the city's gates. In the New Jerusalem, these magnificent angels will proclaim God's goodness as we come and go.

> The twelve gates were made of pearls—each gate from a single pearl! And the main street was pure gold, as clear as glass. (Revelation 21:21)

Each gate consists of a single precious pearl. I'm trying to imagine this in my mind. Remember the parable of Jesus and the "pearl of great price" (Matthew 13:45,46)? Charles Ellicott points out, "The pearl was esteemed of the greatest value among the ancients; it is an appropriate emblem of the highest truth. It is the only precious stone which the art and skill of man cannot improve."[2] Pearls have a beautiful soft luster and glow about them, so these gates must be exquisite. The gates will always be open day or night. There will be coming and going in the New Jerusalem.

> There will be coming and going in the New Jerusalem.

Picture streets paved with brilliant gold, transparent as glass. This golden pavement will be so pure that it is translucent. As beautiful as this may be, its value is nothing compared to Jesus, who loved and died for us.

How will we worship God in the New Heaven?

> I saw no temple in the city, for the Lord God Almighty and the Lamb are its temple. And the city has no need of sun

The Holy City–The New Jerusalem or *(City Girl or Country Girl?)*

or moon, for the glory of God illuminates the city, and the Lamb is its light. (Revelation 21:22, 23)

We will now be living in the complete Kingdom of God. We won't have to worship him at a temple or church. Jesus will walk among us. We'll have instant access to him at any time. Remember the conversation Jesus had with the woman at the well. She asked him,

"Sir, you must be a prophet. So tell me, why is it that you Jews insist that Jerusalem is the only place of worship, while we Samaritans claim it is here at Mount Gerizim, where our ancestors worshiped?" Jesus told her: "Believe me, dear woman, *the time is coming* when it will no longer matter whether you worship the Father on this mountain or in Jerusalem." (John 4:19-21)

The Time is Coming.

The light source in the New Jerusalem will be like none before. Just imagine how people felt when they experienced electricity for the first time. We will be like those people. The light in the New Heavens will come from the very source of the glory of God. It's difficult to envision.

The nations will walk in its light, and the kings of the world will enter the city in all their glory. Its gates will never be closed at the end of the day because there is no night there. And all the nations will bring their glory and honor into the city. Nothing evil will be allowed to enter, nor anyone who practices shameful idolatry and dishonesty—but only those whose names are written in the Lamb's Book of Life. (Revelation 21:24-27)

The above scripture leads me to think that people from all nations will come and go, in and out of the city. "The city's open gates are a great equalizer. There's no elitism in Heaven; everyone will have access because of Christ's blood" (Randy Alcorn).[3] There is much talk today about equity, anti-racism, and equal opportunity. In Heaven, every citizen equally enjoys the wonders of the New Jerusalem. Dwight L. Moody strongly believed "the society of heaven will be select. No one who studies Scripture can doubt that. There are a good many kinds of aristocracy in this world, but the aristocracy of heaven will be the aristocracy of holiness. The humblest sinner on earth will be an aristocrat there."[4]

I have so many questions about the New Jerusalem. Where will we live? How will we get around? Will there be grocery stores, restaurants, and parks? Is there shopping in the city? Is this a place that I want to live? As an introvert, do I want to live next door to millions of people? Do I want to be a country or city girl on the New Earth? So many questions. I need to do more research.

The Holy City–The New Jerusalem or *(City Girl or Country Girl?)*

Light-seeds

Will Heaven be a city? Revelation mentions it 15 times. What is a city? What happens in a city? What will you do in the New Jerusalem? How will the New Jerusalem be different from the cities of today?

Revelation 21:3, 4 says, "Look! God's home is now among his people! No tears, no pain, no sorrow." What will that be like for you?

The City shimmered like a precious gemstone—clean—dazzling—pulsing light! Have you experienced anything even close to this?

The angel is carrying a gold measuring stick to measure the gates and the walls. How do you begin to comprehend the size of the New Jerusalem?

Why would God place a wall around the New Jerusalem?

Imagine walking by an angel as you enter the gates of the city. The angels are proclaiming the Glory of God!

Nothing evil will come in: Imagine

Dwight L. Moody believed that the "aristocracy of Heaven will the aristocracy of holiness. The humblest sinner on earth will be an aristocrat there." Every citizen in Heaven will enjoy it equally. Where do you fall in this aristocracy?

Walk Me Into Heaven

14

I Can Only Imagine

Will I stand in Your presence?
Or to my knees will I fall?
Will I sing hallelujah?
Will I be able to speak at all?
(*I Can Only Imagine*–Mercy Me)[1]

God has given me a vivid imagination. Everything in this chapter is just that—images in my mind—based on scripture. But why not? Why can't we envision the New Jerusalem? What will we do there? Will we sleep? If so, where will we sleep? What about grocery stores and restaurants and parks and animals? Will I dance with Jesus? So many questions. Why do we think that imagining Heaven is somehow not scriptural or biblical? God would not have given John the revelation of Heaven if he hadn't wanted us to know. There is a warning, however, in Chapter 22 to not add to or remove any of these words. But I don't think that bars us from digging deep and asking God to give us a picture of Heaven that we can understand today.

"I do not think that it is wrong for us to think and talk about Heaven. I like to locate Heaven and find out all I can about it. I expect to live there through all eternity. If I were going to dwell in any place in this country, if I were going to make it my home, I would want to inquire about the place, about its climate, about the neighbors I would have, about everything, in fact, that I could learn concerning it." (Dwight L. Moody)[2]

At the Last Supper, Jesus knew that he would soon leave his friends. His disciples had no clue what was about to happen. He wanted to reassure them that he would go and prepare a place for them, but someday he would come back and take them there with him.

> "If it were not so, I would have told you."

Let not your heart be troubled: ye believe in God, believe also in me. In my Father's house are many mansions: if it were not so, I would have told you. I go to prepare a place for you. And if I go and prepare a place for you, I will come again, and receive you unto myself; that where I am, there ye may be also. And whither I go ye know, and the way ye know." (John 14:1-4, KJV)

The disciples would have understood what Jesus meant when he told them he would prepare a place for them. In Jewish culture, a young bride joined the groom's father's household. After the betrothal, the young man returned to his father's house to build a room for himself and his bride. The construction might take over a year or more. After the room was complete, the young man would fetch his bride. She did not know the day or the hour. She prepared for her bridegroom daily, listening and wondering if this was the day. The only warning she would get before the groom's arrival was a trumpet call and a shout.

KJV says there are many mansions. Is this a correct picture of where we will live on the New Earth? Years ago, every Pres-

I Can Only Imagine

byterian church had a "manse" built beside it. This manse or mansion was the home of the preacher and his family. Most of these family members (especially the preacher's kids and wife) would agree that they did not want to live in a "mansion" like that for all eternity. The Greek word here for mansion is *moni*. This word does not reference a large home but means an "abiding or dwelling place."

> Don't let your hearts be troubled. Trust in God, and trust also in me. There is more than enough room in my Father's home. If this were not so, would I have told you that I am going to prepare a place for you? (John 14:1, 2)

Jesus never lies. He assures the disciples that he wouldn't have told them this if it wasn't true. I believe him, too. We will have a "home" or dwelling place on the New Earth. We will not be some spirits floating around, but with our new resurrected bodies, we will have an actual physical residence to live in and call home. We may have a home in New Jerusalem and a home somewhere else on the New Earth. Why not?

> Everything will be familiar yet fresh and new.

The New Jerusalem! Can you picture this city? Will it look modern? Medieval? A cross between the beauty of architecture over the centuries? Everything will be familiar, yet fresh and new.

> "Everything is gone that ever made the old Jerusalem, like all cities, torn apart, dangerous, heartbreaking, seamy. (In the New Jerusalem) you walk the streets in peace now. Small children play unattended in the parks. No stranger goes by whom you can't imagine a fast friend. The city has become what those who loved it always dreamed of and what, in their dreams, it always was, the New Jerusalem. That seems to be the secret of Heaven. The new Chicago, Leningrad, Hiroshima, Baghdad. The new bus driver, hot-dog man, seamstress,

and hairdresser. The new you, me, everybody."
(Frederick Buechner)[3]

Several years ago, I read the incredible story of Captain Dale Black in his book *Flight to Heaven: A Plane Crash...a Lone Survivor...a Journey to Heaven--And Back.* Amazingly, after a horrific plane crash, nineteen-year-old Dale "died" and went to Heaven. He said nothing for several years until he finally shared his experience with his wife and grandfather. Slowly, his story unfolded, and he eventually wrote a book. The following excerpt certainly stirs my imagination.

> "I was fast approaching a magnificent city, golden and gleaming among a myriad of resplendent colors. The light I saw was the purest I had ever seen. And the music was the most majestic, enchanting, and glorious I had ever heard. I was still approaching the city, but now I was slowing down like a plane making its final approach for landing. I knew instantly that this place was entirely and utterly holy. Don't ask me how I knew; I just knew.
>
> I was overwhelmed by its beauty. It was breathtaking. And a strong sense of belonging filled my heart; I never wanted to leave. Somehow, I knew I was made for this place, and this place was made for me . . . The entire city was bathed in light, an opaque whiteness in which the light was intense but diffused. In that dazzling light, every color imaginable seemed to exist and—what's the right word?—played . . . The colors seemed to be alive, dancing in the air. I had never seen so many different colors . . . It was breathtaking to watch. And I could have spent forever doing just that."

I especially love his descriptions of the houses that he saw:

> "Between the central part of the city and the city walls were groupings of brightly colored picture—perfect homes in small, quaint towns . . . Each home was customized and unique from the others yet blended harmoniously. Some were three or four stories; some

were even higher. There were no two the same. If music could become homes, it would look like these, beautifully built and perfectly balanced.."[4]

Captain Black journeyed to the Intermediate Heaven, but how much more wonderful will the New Heaven and the New Jerusalem be for us?

Revelation 22 continues to describe the wonder of the city.

> Then the angel showed me a river with the water of life, clear as crystal, flowing from the throne of God and of the Lamb. It flowed down the center of the main street. On each side of the river grew a tree of life, bearing twelve crops of fruit, with a fresh crop each month. The leaves were used for medicine to heal the nations. (Revelation 22:1, 2)

It's not difficult to imagine this beautiful river. I love Colorado with its mountains, evergreen trees, crystal-clear streams, and brooks. The air is pure and fragrant with notes of pine and fir. You can drink it in. God always gives us a taste of Heaven if we look for it. The beauty of nature does that for me. The New Earth will multiply and magnify the marvels of our present earth. The good news is that we won't have to leave the city and travel a long distance by car or plane to experience the beauty of God's creation. No, this river runs through the heart of the New Jerusalem. The angel showed John a river that flowed with the water of life—crystal clear and thirst-quenching.

Water is life-giving. It is vital for our survival. If we feast on the New Earth, won't we also drink? Jesus told us that he was the Living Water and anyone who drinks of him will never thirst again. I believe that we will literally and figuratively drink from this river. The water will be sweet and satisfying. This beautiful, crystal-clear river flows through the main street of New Jerusalem. Its source is the very throne of God and of the Lamb. I can close my eyes and easily picture picnics with my family (my great-

> Picnics with my family.

great-grandmother?) and friends along its banks. I see children wading in the sparkling water, sailing toy boats, and skipping rocks. Can't you hear their laughter ring out through the park? The temperature will be a perfect 70 degrees, and the warmth and light of God will pulsate and shine through everything. This radiant light will infuse and bathe everything from the inside out. Isaiah 60 describes this glorious light.

> All nations will come to your light;
> mighty kings will come to see your radiance.
> As they apply to Heaven or Hell,
> No longer will you need the sun to shine by day,
> nor the moon to give its light by night,
> for the Lord, your God will be your everlasting light,
> and your God will be your glory.
> Your sun will never set;
> your moon will not go down.
> For the Lord will be your everlasting light.
> Your days of mourning will come to an end.
> (Isaiah 60: 3, 19, 20)

And then John:

> The City doesn't need sun or moon for light. God's Glory is its light, the Lamb its lamp! The nations will walk in its light and earth's kings bring in their splendor. (Revelation 21:23, 24, Message)

But wait—there's more! Thousands of years ago, God gave Ezekiel a vision of the fruit along the banks of the river in the New Jerusalem.

> But the river itself, on both banks, will grow fruit trees of all kinds. Their leaves won't wither, the fruit won't fail. Every month they'll bear fresh fruit because the river from the Sanctuary flows to them. Their fruit will be for food and

I Can Only Imagine

their leaves for healing. (Ezekiel 47:12, Message)

God gave John a similar vision of these trees:

> The Tree of Life was planted on each side of the River, producing twelve kinds of fruit, a ripe fruit each month. The leaves of the Tree are for healing the nations. Never again will anything be cursed. (Revelation 22: 2, Message)

There's no need to bring food to our picnic when we can simply reach up and pick a luscious fruit of the month from one of the trees. This fruit will be like nothing we have ever tasted—sweet, juicy, and fragrant. Imagine a bouquet of perfectly ripe peaches, delicate and floral. My mouth waters just thinking about it. Think of the physical senses (more than five?) in our resurrected bodies, heightened beyond anything we can experience now.

> There will be only God's *shalom.*

As I picture the beauty of this river and the New Jerusalem, I feel a peace that can only come from God. There will be no fear in this City. There will be no evil or distress. There will be only God's shalom. All the tribes will greet each other in peace. There will be no dissension or discord among them. Finally, the leaves of the Trees along the river will bring healing to God's people.

I can only imagine!

Light-seeds

Why do people think imagining Heaven is somehow unscriptural?

Jesus told his disciples at the Last Supper, "Don't let your hearts be troubled. Trust in God, and trust also in me. There is more than enough room in my Father's home" (John 14:1,2). He wanted to reassure them. How does that reassure you?

How do you picture the New Jerusalem? Stores? Houses? Apartments? Parks? Laughing people? Picnics? Family reunions?

Have you ever walked in a pristine forest or waded in a sparkling stream? Felt the warmth of the sun (Son) on your face? Think Heaven. Pure JOY.

15

What's There to Do Forever and Ever and Ever? or (Will We Be Bored on the New Earth?)

"I can safely say, on the authority of all that is revealed in the Word of God, that any man or woman on this earth who is bored and turned off by worship is not ready for heaven." A.W. Tozer[1]

The dictionary defines boredom as wearied by dullness or sameness. Someone once asked Billy Graham this: "I can't imagine living forever and not getting bored. I get bored on Earth, so won't I get bored in Heaven?" Dr. Graham answered, "But one thing is certain: We will not be bored in Heaven! In Heaven, we will be in God's presence forever—and just as He is infinite, the experiences He gives us will be infinite. He also is omniscient (that is, He is limitless in His knowledge), and no matter what we learn in Heaven, there will always be more to discover. I often think of the Apostle Paul's statement: 'Oh, the depth of the riches of the wisdom and knowledge of God! How unsearchable his judgments and his paths beyond tracing out!'" (Romans 11:33).[2]

In the last couple of chapters, I've been talking about the New Earth and the New Jerusalem. I'm sure we won't be bored while waiting in the Intermediate Heaven, but once we get our resurrected bodies, the "sky's the limit!" I can guarantee that the word "bored" will not be in the Heavenly dictionary.

> "Our belief that Heaven will be boring betrays a heresy–that God is boring." RA

Not only will we have the New Jerusalem to explore, but we will also have the entire New Earth and universe. I really can't begin to wrap my brain around that.

> "Our belief that Heaven will be boring betrays a heresy—that God is boring. There's no greater nonsense. What's true is that our desire for pleasure and the experience of joy come directly from God's hand. God designed and gave us our taste buds, adrenaline, sex drives, and the nerve endings that convey pleasure to our brains. Likewise, our imaginations and our capacity for joy and exhilaration were made by the very God we accuse of being boring! Do we imagine that we ourselves came up with the idea of fun?"
> (Randy Alcorn)[3]

God will give us a job or career on the New Earth. I'll talk about that in another chapter, but there will be plenty of time (obviously) to have fun. We've all heard about having a bucket list before we die. There is nothing wrong with traveling and enjoying all the world has to offer. I can think of many things that I would still love to do. But at 75, my body and finances surely curtail most of them.

Some people spend their entire lives chasing after adventures because they believe that today is all they have. I like what Derek Brown says to believers.

> "The pursuit of a bucket list can easily take time and energy away from other priorities and encourage us to focus too much on ourselves. But if we are convinced

that life on the new earth holds opportunities for unimaginable and unsurpassed enjoyment, we will be able to set aside our grand plans for global travel and adventure and give our lives to serving others. This approach to life may not get you a stunning collection of Instagram photos, but you will please your Master and bring joy to others. And that's better than one thousand mountain-top selfies any day."[4]

In his essay, *What Heaven Is*, John McArthur wrote: "Everything we love, value, everything eternal is in Heaven. Nevertheless, the church in this century has tended to be self-indulgent, proof that many Christians have lost their heavenly perspective. Too many don't want to go to Heaven until they've enjoyed all that the world can deliver. Only when all earthly pursuits are exhausted, or when age and sickness hamper their enjoyment, are they ready for Heaven. It is as if they pray, 'Please God, don't take me to heaven yet; I haven't been to Hawaii.'"[5]

> Some people spend their entire lives chasing after adventures because they believe today is all they have.

Several months ago, I watched a trailer from a documentary on Yellowstone National Park by Kevin Costner. He talked about all the things he would miss most when he finally had to "walk away." There were books he had never read, music he had never heard, and stories he wished he had known.[6]

Kevin's words struck me as sad. As he narrated the trailer, his voice had no joy but only a poignancy or sadness about what he would miss. If I could sit down and talk to him, I'd say, "Kevin, this life is not all there is. If I am a Christ-follower, the New Earth will have all the above: books, music, and adventures you can't even imagine! Do you think Yellowstone is fabulous now? Just think what it will look like on the New Earth!"

Walk Me Into Heaven

Will there be adventure and travel on the New Earth? Of course! In my younger years, I loved to travel. I've been all over the world, from Israel to Europe to the Indian Ocean—in planes, trains, automobiles (and even on a motorcycle). I loved the dreaming and planning parts of the trips. What would I enjoy the most? How would I get there? I don't know how we'll get around on the New Earth, but I do know that Jesus, in his resurrected body, just "appeared" from here to there, even walking through walls. The New Earth will have a dimension we cannot access on the Old Earth.

Do I have a heavenly bucket list? Yes, I do. I can only imagine bathing an elephant with my great-grandchildren or if the Lord tarries—my great great grandchildren! Imagine climbing to the top of the tallest tree with them to observe the nest of an eagle. Attending an orchestra concert made up of 1,000 musicians with my two grandsons, Slaton, playing the drums and my grandson, Silas, on the trumpet. Sitting down with Jesus and my son, Shane, and discussing theology–and finally understanding! Running across the Grand Canyon with my daughter-in-law, Stephanie. Snorkeling through a pristine coral reef with my daughter, Stacey, and son-in-law, Robert, and climbing a mountain with my grandson, Preston. Swimming with the dolphins with my granddaughters, Kate and Saylor, and petting a ten-point buck with my grandson, Asher. (Sorry, Asher, there's probably no deer hunting in Heaven.) Cheering my grandson, Patton, as he plays football with Tim Tebow and his great-granddad, Ray—imagine! What would it be like to take a jeep trip with my daughter, Starr, and son-in-law, Blake, to the top of the highest mountain to catch one of a million (+) gorgeous sunsets? How much fun to hike the most breathtaking national parks with my husband, Preston—no huffing and puffing.

My heavenly bucket list.

Won't it be fun to sit around the table with all my Bible study sisters over the years, digging into God's word as we had never been able to do before? Fly fishing with my daddy and Grandmother Smith, wading in a sparkling mountain stream. I

What's There to Do Forever and Ever and Ever . . . ?

can see my mother and me sitting together, sewing or crocheting something beautiful. I can hear her laughter even now. Walking through a completely restored Israel with my sweet mother-in-law will be amazing. And then I might take long walks with my grandmothers and grandfathers from the past. Fancy that!

Randy Alcorn's wife, Nanci, died in March 2022, making all this real to the man who authored the book *Heaven*. Several years ago, he wrote about their heavenly bucket list.

"Perhaps an alarm is going off—but that's unspiritual—we should only want to be with Jesus. Well, Jesus is right at the top of both of our post-bucket lists! Would the same God who says we should eat and drink to his glory (1 Cor. 10:31) be offended if we want to play with his animals for his glory and travel to the stars for his glory?"

Alcorn continues:

"For the Christian, death is not the end of the adventure, but our exit from a world where dreams and adventures shrink, and entrance into a world where dreams and adventures forever expand. Heaven will be full of activities that are designed specifically for our enjoyment by God."[7]

Yes! Above all, I can only imagine spending time with Jesus as we walk along the shores of a sparkling lake nestled high in the mountains. I can close my eyes and see that water shimmering like a thousand sapphires. As we stop to skip rocks (a skill I was terrible at in my old life), we laugh until tears come to our eyes—only tears of joy in Heaven. I'm finally able to see my Lord face to face and ask him questions that have so long been in my heart. Thinking about it now as I write these words puts a smile on my face and anticipation in my spirit. Will Heaven be boring? No way!

Will art or crafting exist in the New Jerusalem and the New Earth? Why not? In Exodus, God charged a man named Bezalel, son of Uri, to use his skills, abilities, and knowledge in all kinds of crafts to build the Tabernacle.

Then the Lord said to Moses, "Look, I have specifically chosen Bezalel son of Uri, grandson of Hur, of the tribe of Judah. I have *filled him with the Spirit of God*, giving him great wisdom, ability, and expertise in all kinds of crafts. He is a master craftsman and an expert in working with gold, silver, and bronze. He is skilled in engraving and mounting gemstones and in carving wood. He is a master at every craft!
And I have personally appointed Oholiab, son of Ahisamach, of the tribe of Dan, to be his assistant. Moreover, I have given special skill to all the gifted craftsmen so they can make all the things I have commanded you to make." (Exodus 31:1-6)

Some scholars believe that Bezalel was the first person filled with the Spirit. He wasn't a priest or a prophet but a craftsman. How cool is that? For those of you who love textiles, sewing, crocheting, knitting, or quilting, can you even imagine what beautiful works of art you might create?

The Lord gave the craftsmen in Exodus special skills as engravers, designers, embroiderers in blue, purple, and scarlet thread on fine linen cloth, and weavers. They excelled as craftsmen and designers. (Exodus 35:35)

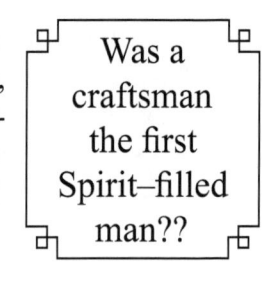

> Was a craftsman the first Spirit–filled man??

Jesus was said to be a craftsman. Some say he didn't necessarily work with wood but with stone. "Is not this the carpenter's son? Is not his mother called Mary" (Matthew 13:55)? The Greek word for carpenter is *tekton* which translates as craftsman or builder. Did he work with wood? Possibly, but there weren't many trees in Nazareth then.

I've seen stunning textiles, crafts, and works of art in museums. I believe the art in the New Earth won't be in museums but

What's There to Do Forever and Ever and Ever . . . ?

in everyone's homes. Those who love sewing, crafting, painting, woodworking, or photography will fill their rooms with exquisite designs that glorify God. No interior designer today can possibly dream of the designs filling these homes.

And then there's photography! As an amateur photographer, my creative juices come alive when I think of the stunning photos I can take on the New Earth. Going on photo shoots anywhere in the world or universe will be so much fun.

What about music? Will there be music on the New Earth? No doubt. All through the scriptures, it is evident that God loves music. Scripture references music between 800 to 1500 times. "Be filled with the Holy Spirit, singing psalms and hymns and spiritual songs among yourselves, and making music to the Lord in your hearts" (Ephesians 5:19). David praised God with the harp and the lyre. He shouted for joy and sang praises to God (Psalm 71:22, 23).

I believe God enjoys all kinds of music—harps, drums, trumpets, and tambourines (Yeah, those too.) Scriptures speak of quiet music like strings and flutes and loud, clamorous music that is thunderous like a ram's horns and clanging symbols. A rock or country music concert can't even compare.

> Praise the Lord!
> Praise God in his sanctuary;
> praise him in his mighty Heaven!
> Praise him for his mighty works;
> praise his unequaled greatness!
> Praise him with a blast of the ram's horn;
> praise him with the lyre and harp!
> Praise him with the tambourine and dancing;
> praise him with strings and flutes!
> Praise him with a clash of cymbals;
> praise him with loud clanging cymbals.
> Let everything that breathes sing praises to the Lord!
> (Psalm 150)

Walk Me Into Heaven

We will witness a myriad—thousands upon thousands—of angels singing like in Revelation 5:11-12.

> Then I looked again, and I heard the voices of thousands and millions of angels around the throne and of the living beings and the elders. And they sang in a mighty chorus:
> "Worthy is the Lamb who was slaughtered—
> to receive power and riches
> and wisdom and strength
> and honor and glory and blessing."

How often can I say, "No, Heaven will not be boring!"

If there's music, will there be dancing in Heaven? Why not? David danced before the Lord (2 Samuel 6:14). Jeremiah speaks of taking up your tambourines and dancing merrily with the joyful (Jeremiah 31:4, 5). Solomon writes about a time to mourn and a time to dance (Ecclesiastics 3:4). There will be no mourning in the New Earth, only dancing. "You have turned my mourning into dancing" (Psalm 30:11). Scriptures admonish us to praise his name with dancing accompanied by a tambourine and harp (Psalm 149:3).

> **No! Heaven will not be boring.**

I'm sure Jesus joined in the dancing at the wedding in Cana. Can't you see him? Round and round in the circle, his head is thrown back, he's singing at the top of his lungs, and he is laughing. Just thinking about this makes me smile. If the people had only known they were dancing with the Lord of the Universe! I can't wait to dance the *Hora* with Jesus—*Hava Nagila* (Let us rejoice).

This song is often sung at funerals: *Lord of the Dance*.
"Dance, then, wherever you may be,
I am the Lord of the dance, said he,
And I'll lead you all, wherever you may be,
And I'll lead you all in the dance, said he."[8]

My last question—will there be sports in Heaven? There *was* the *Field of Dreams* with Kevin Costner—obviously not very biblically correct. Sometimes sports bring out the worst in

What's There to Do Forever and Ever and Ever . . . ?

people—think little league parents. But sports also bring out the best in people. Will there be competition in the New Earth? God placed the need to play in all of us. Paul talks about "running the race," so I think he had attended track events. I don't know. But perhaps God will allow us to create new and even more exciting sports that we can enjoy in our new resurrected (never tiring) bodies. Why not?

Will eternity be boring? Anthony Hoekema writes:
"The possibilities that now rise before us boggle the mind. Will there be better Beethovens on the new earth? . . . better Rembrandts, better Raphaels? Shall we read better poetry, better drama, and better prose? Will scientists continue to advance in technological achievement, will geologists continue to dig out the treasures of the earth, and will architects continue to build imposing and attractive structures? Will there be exciting new adventures in space travel? . . . Our culture will glorify God in ways that surpass our most fantastic dreams."[9]

No, Kevin, eternity will *not* be boring. All those books you've never read, and the music you've never heard, and the stories you've never told, all those things and more are waiting for those who know Jesus as Lord because:

> That is what the Scriptures mean when they say,
> No eye has seen, no ear has heard,
> and no mind has imagined
> what God has prepared
> for those who love him. (1 Corinthians 2:9)

Light-seeds

Be honest: have you ever had the thought, "What's there to do for ever and ever and ever in Heaven?"

"Too many don't want to go to Heaven until they've enjoyed all that the world has to offer." Are we earthly focused or heavenly focused?

Will there be adventure and travel on the New Earth?

What is your Heavenly Bucket list?

16

(RIP) Rest in Peace? or (WIP) Work in Peace?

Several years ago, a dear friend died, and several people wrote *RIP* on her Facebook page. Mulling over that expression, I wrote this in my blog, *Experiencing the Light*.

"This morning, as I mourn yet another friend, I think about the popular epitaph, "RIP" that people often share in consolation. Something just doesn't seem right about that when I think about Heaven. I can't see my friend "resting." She was always busy doing something, teaching the children in her sweet, quiet way, or traveling with her husband."[1]

Will we rest in peace on the New Earth? There will be plenty of peace, true, but rest? Our resurrected bodies won't need physical rest as they do now. There will be a lot of downtime on the New Earth, but God will also assign us purposeful work. "The Lord God placed the man in the Garden of Eden to tend and watch over it (Genesis 2:15). The word "tend" comes from the Greek word "*avodah*," which means "to work." (Interestingly enough, the word "*avodah*" also means "to worship and to serve").

This was a joy, not a curse until Adam and Eve sinned and were forced out of the garden (Genesis 3:17, 23). At that point, work became drudgery. In Revelation 22:3 (NIV), God promises that there will "no longer be a curse. The throne of God and of the Lamb will be in the city, and his servants will serve him" (work for him.) Jesus found satisfaction in work. When the Jewish leaders harassed him for breaking the Sabbath, he told them, "My Father is always working, and so am I" (John 5:17). We are image bearers; therefore, work is a good thing.

In many ways, life today is much simpler than my grandmother's life and those before her. We have so many modern appliances that make our lives physically easier. I can imagine that my grandmother, who raised five kids without disposable diapers, didn't relish going to Heaven and having to work. This poem may speak for her:

> "Here lies a poor woman who was always tired,
> She lived in a house where help wasn't hired:
> Her last words on earth were: 'Dear friends, I am going
> To where there's no cooking, or washing, or sewing,
> For everything there is exact to my wishes,
> For where they don't eat there's no washing of dishes.
> I'll be where loud anthems will always be ringing,
> But having no voice I'll be quit of the singing.
> Don't mourn for me now, don't mourn for me never,
> I am going to do nothing forever and ever." (Anonymous)[2]

Hopefully, God will give that poor woman a job on the New Earth that will be anything but cooking, washing, or sewing.

Theologians argue over when the 1,000-year or Millennial reign of Christ begins. There are amillennialists, postmillennialists, and premillennialists. Oh, my goodness. Each scholar has scriptural "proof" that they are right. I believe that after Jesus returns to earth with the saints (in our resurrected bodies), God will give us (specific to our skills) an essential job during the 1,000 years. Working for the God of the Universe will be richly

(RIP) Rest in Peace? or (WIP) Work in Peace?

fulfilling and purposeful.

On the New Earth, we won't need doctors, nurses, dentists (thankfully!), counselors, psychologists, wheelchair manufacturers, garbage collectors, electricians, undertakers, pharmacists, soldiers, politicians (Heaven is a theocracy), law enforcement, insurance agents, bankers, lawyers, social workers; the list goes on and on.

> *No Dentists on the New Earth!*

Many people today work at an unfulfilling and laborious job—actual drudgery. But some are blessed with a job that gives them joy and a sense of accomplishment. Many times, our attitudes determine our success. God promises that the career he provides us on the New Earth will be rewarding and satisfying. How can it not be? I read this in Gotquestions.org:

> "In our current world, we have this command: 'Whatever you do, work at it with all your heart, as working for the Lord' (Colossians 3:23). The work that Christians perform in Heaven will have the same goal: to be an act of worship glorifying the Lord. The difference will be that, in eternity, the work that God has prepared for us will be instantly rewarding, constantly refreshing, and perfectly suited for whom we were created to be."[3]

During the Millennium, God will appoint some to rule. These people may be a surprise to us. Jesus speaks of those given unique talents in Matthew 25:14-30 and Luke 19:12-28. What had these people accomplished during their lifetimes with these talents? Perhaps those who have served faithfully on earth will be given jobs accordingly. "If you are faithful in little things, you will be faithful in large ones" (Luke 16:10). Jesus said, "For those who exalt themselves will be humbled, and those who humble themselves will be exalted" (Luke 14:11).

The prophets like Amos and Isaiah foretold some of our careers on the New Earth.

Some jobs will be in the field of agriculture:

Walk Me Into Heaven

"The time will come," says the Lord,
"when the grain and grapes will grow faster
  than they can be harvested.
  Then the terraced vineyards on the hills of Israel
  will drip with sweet wine!
  I will bring my exiled people of Israel
  back from distant lands,
  and they will rebuild their ruined cities
  and live in them again.
  They will plant vineyards and gardens;
  they will eat their crops and drink their wine.
  I will firmly plant them there
  in their own land.
  They will never again be uprooted
  from the land I have given them,"
  says the Lord your God. (Amos 9:13-15)

Some might be merchants.

Your eyes will shine,
and your heart will thrill with joy,
for merchants from around the world will come to you.
They will bring you the wealth of many lands.
(Isaiah 60:5)

Since "nation will no longer fight against nation nor train for war anymore," some might:

Hammer their swords into plowshares
and their spears into pruning hooks. (Isaiah 2:4)

And then some might be builders of homes.

Some of you will rebuild the deserted ruins of your cities.
Then you will be known as a rebuilder of walls
and a restorer of homes. (Isaiah 58:12)

(RIP) Rest in Peace? or (WIP) Work in Peace?

In those days, people will live in the houses they build and eat the fruit of their own vineyards. (Isaiah 65:21)

God is the Creator, the Designer, the Inventor, the Maker, and the Originator. Since we are image-bearers, he has placed the desire to create within us. Here on earth, our creativity is limited in many ways. On the New Earth, God will bless our lives and jobs with inspiration and brilliance beyond our imagination. God will design and assign as many creative jobs as there are unique and distinct servants on the New Earth.

> God has placed the desire to create within us.

John J. Burdette was a Baptist minister, humorist, and writer. He served as a private in the Civil War and later wrote a humorous column for the Peoria Daily Transcript. His column became popular throughout the country. He wrote this: "My work is about ended. I think the best of it I have done poorly; any of it I might have done better; but I have done it. And in a fairer land, with finer material and a better working light, I shall so do a better work. Yes, a much better work."[4] I love how he mentions a better working light. At my age, I so understand that!

We will be God's servants on the New Earth. Charles Spurgeon (1834-1892), the Prince of Preachers, often wrote of Heaven. He penned this about being servants on the New Earth:

> "What engagements we may have throughout eternity we are not told, because we have enough to do to fulfill out engagements now; but assuredly we shall be honored with errands of mercy and tasks of love fitted for our heavenly being; and I doubt not it shall be one of our greatest delights while seeing the Lord's face to serve him with all our perfected powers. He will use us in the grand economy of future manifestations of his divine glory. Possibly we may be to other dispensations what the angels have been to this. Be that as it may, we shall find a part of our bliss and joy in constantly serving

him who has raised us from the dead."[5]

Our occupation in Heaven will directly correlate with our interests and dreams on earth. Our work on the New Earth will be creative and over and above anything we can accomplish now. We will never be bored, jaded, or impatient with it. For many years, W.A. Criswell was pastor of the largest Baptist Church in the world, First Baptist Church in Dallas, Texas. He loved his job and believed he would continue it on the New Earth. He wrote:

> "In our work, we shall administer, according to the Word of God, the entire universe and everything that is in it. That includes God's solar system and the infinitude of the world about us. The government of the universe will be given into our hands, and the administration of God's creation will be turned over to us."[6]

The universe? Oh, my goodness. That's very difficult for me to visualize—working throughout God's universe.

What will work look like on the New Earth? For one thing, it will not be driven or limited by finances or resources. Even now on the present Earth, "This same God who takes care of me will supply all your needs from his glorious riches, which have been given to us in Christ Jesus" (Philippians 4:19). How much more so on the New Earth? Whatever resources we need for our jobs will be abundantly provided by God's *glorious riches*. Let's say you work on the New Earth as an artist; God will provide only the finest premium paints in myriad unique colors, some wholly fresh and original, to the New Earth. Carpenters and builders will have lovely, fine-grained woods to build homes and furniture. The sweet fragrance of these timbers will waft from their shops as you walk by. God will provide seamstresses with luxurious fine linens and textiles to design and sew the clothes that we will wear.

Farmers will have only the finest farmland, seeds, and equipment. "Then the Lord will bless you with rain at planting time. There will be wonderful harvests and plenty of pastureland for your livestock" (Isaiah 30:23). Fishermen will fish pristine waters in magnificent vessels, even those waters that were once dead on the old Earth. "Fishermen will stand along the shores of the Dead

(RIP) Rest in Peace? or (WIP) Work in Peace?

Sea. All the way from En-gedi to En-eglaim, the shores will be covered with nets drying in the sun. Fish of every kind will fill the Dead Sea, just as they fill the Mediterranean" (Ezekiel 47:10).

Work on the New Earth will be totally enjoyable! In his book, *The Heaven Life*, David Gregg, a Presbyterian minister, wrote about work on the New Earth. His take on work in Heaven is very contemporary. He wrote:

> "It is work as free from care and toil and fatigue as is the wing-stroke of the jubilant lark when it soars into the sunlight of a fresh, clear day and, spontaneously and for self-relief, pours out its thrilling carol. Work up there is a matter of self-relief, as well as a matter of obedience to the ruling will of God. It is work according to one's tastes and delight and ability. If tastes vary there, then occupations will also vary there."[7]

There will be no deadlines, unreasonable bosses, stress, and (above all) sin that affects work here on earth. There will be no "dead-end" jobs on the New Earth. Every job that God provides will be for a specific purpose and an appointed role in his Kingdom.

Finally, and most importantly, God will appoint some to serve him by ruling on the New Earth. In Revelation 5:9, 10, the four living creatures and twenty-four elders who surround God's throne say to Jesus:

> You are worthy to take the scroll and break its seals and open it. For you were slaughtered, and your blood has ransomed people for God from every tribe and language and people and nation. And you have caused them to become a Kingdom of priests for our God. And they will reign on the earth.

> If we endure hardship,
> we will reign with him. (2 Timothy 2:12)

Daniel had a vision of God's people reigning with him.

Then the sovereign, power, and greatness of all the kingdoms under heaven will be given to the holy people of the Most High. His kingdom will last forever, and all rulers will serve and obey him. (Daniel 7:27)

God says: "To all who are victorious, who obey me to the very end, to them I will give authority over all the nations." (Revelation 2:26)

This morning I read Genesis 11 about the Tower of Babel. The people decided to build a great city and a tower that reached (according to them) Heaven. Unfortunately, they purposed to make a name for themselves and become powerful. God saw through their sin, confused their language, and scattered them across the face of the earth. On the New Earth, everyone will again have the same language, enabling God's people to rule the nations with his peace and love.

Yes, we will *work in peace (WIP)* on the New Earth. Our jobs will be specifically ordained by God and used to continue his kingdom into all eternity. Now that's job security!

I hope my headstone reads WIP and not RIP.

(RIP) Rest in Peace? or (WIP) Work in Peace?

Light-seeds

We will serve (work) for God. How important is it to you to have a job on the New Earth?

Working for the God of the Universe will be richly rewarding! What job would you like to do? Not like to do?

Have you thought about there being farmers, merchants, carpenters, etc., on the New Earth? Or do you think God provides everything for us?

What will work look like in the New Earth? As an artist? A musician? A carpenter? A farmer? ???

Walk Me Into Heaven

17

It's Resurrection, Resurrection, Always Resurrection
(No Botox Needed)

Social Media was in a tizz. Madonna (definitely not Jesus' mother) performed at the Grammys. She was almost unrecognizable. She responded to the criticism by saying, "I'm caught in the glare of ageism and misogyny." She also claimed that the long-lens camera distorted her face. It seems sad to me. Millions or billions of dollars are spent today in the cosmetic surgery industry. Women and men seek to recapture the face and body of their youth. The Word of God has such good news. As Christ-followers, we may go to our graves with wrinkled and withered bodies, but God promises that we will someday rise with a new, fresh, resurrected body! Paul describes it brilliantly:

> This image of planting a dead seed and raising a live plant is a mere sketch at best, but perhaps it will help in approaching the mystery of the resurrection body—but only if you keep in mind that when we're raised, we're raised for good, alive forever! The corpse that's planted is no beauty, but when it's raised, it's glorious. Put in the ground weak, it comes up powerful. The seed sown is natural; the seed grown is

supernatural—same seed, same body, but what a difference from when it goes down in physical mortality to when it is raised up in spiritual immortality. (1 Corinthians 15:42-44, Message)

Our resurrected body will never experience decay, sickness, decline, or, best yet—wrinkles! Every morning as I wake up and squint in the mirror, I wonder who that person is. God promises that someday he will restore my old, aching body to when I was young and healthy. Here's the thing—as a follower of Christ, do I really, genuinely believe that God raised Jesus from the dead? Yes. I do. Unfortunately, some "Christians" today don't think that is important. Not believing in the resurrection is nothing new.

But tell me this—since we preach that Christ rose from the dead, why are some of you saying there will be no resurrection of the dead? For if there is no resurrection of the dead, then Christ has not been raised either. And if Christ has not been raised, then all our preaching is useless, and your faith is useless. And we apostles would all be lying about God—for we have said that God raised Christ from the grave. But that can't be true if there is no resurrection of the dead. And if there is no resurrection of the dead, then Christ has not been raised. And if Christ has not been raised, then your faith is useless and you are still guilty of your sins. (1 Corinthians 15:12-17)

"But tell me this."

There needs to be a bumper sticker that says, "It's All About the Resurrection." Yes, as Christ-followers, God assists and guides us through this life to live it more abundantly, but if Jesus had not died and been resurrected, Christianity would just have been another "moral" and dead religion. The FACT is that Roman soldiers and the Jewish authorities crucified Jesus; he died and came back to life! If Jesus' mortal body returned to life, those who believed would also live forever. That is God's promise. There

It's Resurrection, Resurrection, Always Resurrection

have been many books written about the resurrection. Researchers and theologians have dug deep into scriptures and history to come up with the fact that, yes, the resurrection is true. Would people die for a lie? Here is an interesting quote from Chuck Colson: "I know the resurrection is a fact, and Watergate proved it to me. How? Because 12 men testified they had seen Jesus raised from the dead, then they proclaimed that truth for 40 years, never once denying it. Everyone was beaten, tortured, stoned, and put in prison. They would not have endured that if it weren't true. Watergate embroiled 12 of the most powerful men in the world—and they couldn't keep a lie for three weeks. You're telling me 12 apostles could keep a lie for 40 years? Absolutely impossible."[1]

Paul reaffirms that he would not die for a lie.

And why do you think I keep risking my neck in this dangerous work? I look death in the face practically every day I live. Do you think I'd do this if I wasn't convinced of your resurrection and mine as guaranteed by the resurrected Messiah Jesus? Do you think I was just trying to act heroic when I fought the wild beasts at Ephesus, hoping it wouldn't be the end of me? Not on your life! It's resurrection, resurrection, always resurrection, that undergirds what I do and say, the way I live. If there's no resurrection, "We eat, we drink, the next day we die," and that's all there is to it. But don't fool yourselves. Don't let yourselves be poisoned by this anti-resurrection loose talk. "Bad company ruins good manners." (1 Corinthians 15:30-33, Message)

> Who would die for a lie?

What does the resurrection mean to me? To my family? To my friends? What will my resurrected body be like? It will not be a "new" body but a "renewed" body. According to the Cambridge Dictionary, "resurrected from the dead" means "The act of bringing something that had disappeared or ended back into use or existence."

> Our earthly bodies are planted in the ground when we die, but they will be raised to live forever. Our bodies are buried in brokenness, but they will be raised in glory. They are buried in weakness, but they will be raised in strength. (1 Corinthians 15:42, 43)

God will not start from scratch with our newly improved bodies. Paul says that our bodies will be "raised," meaning that God will raise our current earthly bodies in glory and strength.

When I look in the mirror on the New Earth, I will see and recognize myself—a short, "younger" woman with blonde hair (hopefully thicker this time), blue eyes (no glasses), and the same skin color. There will be people of all sizes, shapes, and skin colors. None of that will matter on the New Earth.

Randy Frazee describes the diverse New Earth in is book, *What Happens After You Die: A Biblical Guide to Paradise, Hell, and Life After Death:*

> "We live in a time of great racial tension. It has always been this way; it shall always be this way until this old world comes to an end and Jesus returns. On the New Earth, we will not all look or sound the same. Diversity will still exist, but we will be completely unified. How can this be? In our diversity, we will experience unity under the name of Jesus, who sits on the throne. It will be a beautiful thing."[2]

Paul concurs:

> You will notice that the variety of bodies is stunning. Just as there are different kinds of seeds, there are different kinds of bodies—humans, animals, birds, fish—each unprecedented in its form. You get a hint at the diversity of resurrection glory by looking at the diversity of bodies not only on earth but in the skies—sun, moon, stars—all these varieties of beauty

and brightness. And we're only looking at pre-resurrection "seeds"—who can imagine what the resurrection "plants" will be like! (1 Corinthians 15:39-41, Message)

When we look at Jesus' resurrected body, we understand what our resurrected bodies will be like.

We're waiting for the arrival of the Savior, the Master, Jesus Christ, who will transform our earthly bodies into glorious bodies *like his own*. He'll make us beautiful and whole with the same powerful skill by which he is putting everything as it should be, under and around him. (Philippians 3:20, 21, Message)

After Jesus was raised from the dead, he appeared first to Mary Magdalene at the tomb. Mary recognized him only once he spoke to her. Since it was just daylight, he may have been across the garden from her. She was not expecting to see Jesus alive. But, hearing his voice, she knew! "Don't cling to me, for I have not yet ascended to the Father" (John 20:17, Message). I don't think Mary gave Jesus a gentle hug. I think she grabbed him and didn't want to let go. Wouldn't you have? He was no ghost or spirit; Jesus had a body she could touch. I can picture Jesus holding her close and then gently prying her away. He looked into her eyes and explained that he had much to accomplish before he left Earth and returned to Heaven. He instructed her to tell the brothers what had happened.

The next time Jesus appeared was on the road to Emmaus. He walked alongside two men who were discussing all the events of the weekend. Like Mary, these two men didn't recognize him. Could his appearance be veiled from them? Scholars aren't sure. But when they arrived at the house where they were staying, they invited him in for supper (Luke 24:28-31). They recognized him as soon as he sat down and broke the bread. I can see him smiling at them and then disappearing.

Luke records that after the two men left Emmaus, they went

up to Jerusalem. "They found the eleven and their companions gathered together. They were saying to each other, 'The Lord really has risen! He appeared to Simon'" (Luke 24:33, 34). Paul also records this meeting in 1 Corinthians 15:5.

Somewhere in there, Jesus had a one-on-one with Peter. This same Peter turned his back on Jesus and denied knowing him. Can you imagine Peter's face (the relief he felt) when he saw Jesus alive?

Jesus appeared next to the eleven disciples. They had huddled behind closed doors in fear of the Jews. Everyone gathered there except Thomas and (of course) Judas. Suddenly, Jesus materialized before them. Wide-eyed, jaws dropped; they were awestruck (John 20:20). He showed them the nail scars on his hands and feet to prove it was he. Inhaling deeply and audibly, he breathed on them and said, "Receive the Holy Spirit." When they told Thomas about seeing Jesus, he didn't believe them. Scoffing, he said, "Unless I see the nail holes in his hands, put my finger in the nail holes, and stick my hand in his side, I won't believe it" (John 20:25, Message).

> Eight days later, the disciples were together again, and this time Thomas was with them. The doors were locked; but suddenly, as before, Jesus was standing among them. (John 20:26)

Even though they had already encountered Jesus, they still feared the Jews. Notice that John made a point to let us know that although the doors were locked, Jesus (somehow) appeared.

> Then he told Thomas, "Put your finger here and look at my hands. Put your hand into the wound in my side. Don't be faithless any longer. Believe!" (John 20:27)

Thomas gingerly touched the nail marks still on his hands and the wound on his side. I often wonder why Jesus' hands still showed these wounds. The famous preacher, Charles Spurgeon,

It's Resurrection, Resurrection, Always Resurrection

wrote in 1859:

> "It was to establish his identity, that he was the very same Jesus whom they had followed, whom at last they had deserted, whom they had beheld afar off crucified and slain, and whom they had carried to the tomb in the gloom of the evening; it was the very same Christ who was now before them, and they might know it, for there was the seal of his sufferings upon him. He was the same person; the hands and feet could testify to that."[3]

> **Why did he still have the nail scars in his hands?**

As we say today, this flesh-and-bone Jesus was "the real deal."

After this, the disciples traveled to Galilee. Hours before the soldiers arrested Jesus, he gave the disciples these instructions: "After I am raised up, I, your Shepherd, will go ahead of you, leading the way to Galilee" (Matthew 26:32, Message). He met them there, along with *more than* 500 witnesses who saw him simultaneously (1 Corinthians 15:6). Paul later tells the skeptical Corinthians or (Greeks) that some of these people are still alive. Ask them for yourselves!

Jesus appeared to Peter and six other disciples on the shores of the Sea of Galilee. Since they were back in Galilee, they decided to go fishing. A man from the beach called out to them to throw their net on the right-hand side of the boat. Hmm. Something seemed familiar about that. Immediately, Peter recognized that voice! He jumped out of the boat and swam to shore. Can't you picture it? I bet Peter grabbed hold of Jesus, squeezed the fire out of him, and lifted him off his feet—pure joy. Afterward, Jesus cooked a delicious breakfast of fresh fish.

1 Corinthians 15:7 records that Jesus also appeared to his brother, James, the very brother who had no use for him and thought he had lost his mind (Mark 3:21). Imagining this, I wrote a story about James several years ago. He was in Galilee and had just heard that his brother, Jesus, had been crucified.

My numbed mind refused to think as I made my way

up that familiar hill. I tripped once, falling to my knees, numb even to that pain. I stood there momentarily, catching my breath, then stumbled back up and continued walking. Finally, at the top, I sat down heavily on the same boulder that Jesus and I had sat on so many times before. The sun peeked out of the horizon, dusting the valley with a soft, golden light. I stared at the sun, hardly blinking, my thoughts as motionless as my eyes.

Suddenly, as I gazed toward the rising sun, out of the rays of light, I saw an apparition walking toward me. Slowly blinking, I tried to make sense of what I was seeing. I couldn't move; I froze. Could it be? No, this was impossible . . .

And then his voice said, "James."

I slowly stood up, stunned and bewildered.

Shaking my head and mouthing his name, I asked, "Jesus?"

"Yes, my brother, I am alive."

I looked at him again, still not believing my eyes. "You're alive! Jesus, how can this be?"

He walked toward me, smiling, his arms outstretched.

With a loud shout that echoed throughout the valley, I ran to my brother, grabbed hold of him, and hugged him.

"You're alive! You're alive! Still holding on to him, I backed away at arm's length and looked at his beloved face. Laughing at me, he said, "Yes, little brother, I am very much alive." With a whoop, I ran to the cliff's edge, threw back my head, and shouted to the valley below, "He's alive! He's alive!"

Suddenly, I knew. It all made sense now. I fell to my knees and cried out, "Lord Jesus!" Tears streamed down my face as the truth flooded over me. Jesus, my brother Jesus, is the Messiah![4]

The miraculous had happened. Do I believe this? Yes. His resurrected body was flesh and bone (Luke 24:37-39). He could

It's Resurrection, Resurrection, Always Resurrection

be touched and felt (Matthew 28:9, John 20:27). Jesus ate right before them (Luke 24:41). His disciples recognized him. They did not doubt that he was Jesus (Luke 24:13-35). They saw the nail scars on his hands (John 20:19-28). Another time Jesus appeared to the eleven, they were having another meal together. At that time, he told them to wait ten more days in Jerusalem so that they may receive the power of the Holy Spirit (Acts 1:4-5).

> Do I believe this?

The disciples were still puzzled. They had experienced firsthand the bodily resurrection of their Lord. If he could do that, what else could he accomplish? Scriptures say that they kept asking Jesus, obviously more than one time, if he would now restore the kingdom of Israel. Indeed, if he could walk through walls, he could do that. I can see the look of love on his face; soon enough, they would understand. Did Jesus go from man to man and give each a farewell hug and blessing? We don't know. I want to think each man embraced their flesh and blood Lord one more time. Then, to their astonishment, he began to rise off the ground. Stunned and amazed, they watched him defy gravity, "gazing at the Lord lifting above the clouds," and slowly ascend into Heaven. How? Where was he going? What? We don't know how long they stood there and watched him, but the scriptures say that after a time, two angels appeared and told them Jesus would come back to earth in the same way they saw him leave (Mark 16:19-20, Luke 24:50-53, Acts 1:9-11).

God promises that we will also have a resurrected body on the New Earth, just like Jesus'. Here's the promise:

> Our citizenship is in Heaven. We look forward to a savior that comes from there—the Lord Jesus Christ. He will transform our humble bodies so that they are like his glorious body, by the power that also makes him able to subject all things to himself. (Philippians 3:20, 21)

No Botox is needed.

Walk Me Into Heaven

Light-seeds

Why is belief in the resurrection of the dead non-negotiable if you are a Christ-follower?

Who would die for a lie?

God will not start from scratch. Paul says our bodies will be "raised," How do you understand that?

What could Jesus do in his resurrected body?

Why did he still have the nail scars on his hands?

Do you believe that Jesus rose from the dead?

Imagine standing with the disciples and watching Jesus ascend into the clouds.

Have you ever gazed at the gorgeous evening or morning sky and wished to see Jesus ascend from Heaven?

18

Are Max, Bella, and Jazz in Heaven?

Our family loves animals, especially dogs. Holidays are always fun, crazy, and chaotic, with all our dogs running here and there. Leave them at home? Of course not! They're family. Sadly, we have lost three precious pets in the last year and a half.

Jazz, the Brittany Spaniel, was our granddog. She had beautiful, expressive brown eyes. Jazz was pure love; there wasn't a mean bone in her body. She adored my oldest daughter and rarely left her side. Jazz also loved to sit at the front door window and watch for the pesky rabbit to run by, tempting her—enticing her to the chase. How dare that rabbit come into her yard. Of course, it was all a dream, but Jazz never gave up hope that the door would open one day, and she could happily chase that little critter down the street.

Max was my beloved long-haired dachshund. He was my faithful companion for fourteen years. We went through a lot together. In 2012, Max hung with me as I fought through breast cancer. He never left my side. Max would sit and look at me with his beautiful brown eyes. One time, jokingly, I asked my husband if he loved me as much as Max did. Max didn't require anything from me but food, water, and my presence. In the last year of Max's life, he couldn't see or hear but he stayed close to my side. Now it was time for me to be there for Max like he was there for me. He trusted me. Our wonderful vet, Julianne, gently helped Max leave this life as Preston and I stroked his soft red head and ears for the last time. My son, Shane, and grandson, Asher, were there for me when we returned home. They buried Max in our backyard alongside Miss Ruby and Bear. Asher gave me a gentle hug. It's hard. Those of you who have animals know.

Bella was our other granddog. She was a 100-plus pound Harlequin Great Dane. Bella was—BIG! She didn't know that she was a dog. She loved her family, my son, daughter-in-law, and their two boys fiercely, taking care of them, always with her nose in their business. At the end of her life, her humans gave her two new siblings to take care of—Banjo, the Boykin Spaniel puppy, and Maz, the cat. Banjo tended to bug Bella, but Maz loved to curl up beside Bella's big body and nap. Because of their size, Great Danes don't usually have a very long life. One icy, cold evening several months ago, the family sat on the couch in the den watching TV. Nearby, Bella, dressed in her warm red sweater, was curled up on her big bed by the fire. She started panting, and my daughter-in-law sat beside her to stroke her head. Bella took two big breaths and then peacefully died.

Are Max, Jazz, and Bella in Heaven? I don't know. Through the years, I have loved our family pets. We had Herman, Misty, Zipper, Sooner, Sammy, Miss Ellie, Ruby, Max, Bear, and now, Wynna and Rosie. And then there were our cats Julie, Billy Bob, Tess, and Blu (or Wild Man). God created them for our pleasure and delight. I've often thanked him for this. I have a new puppy now. What was I thinking? Just a part of me needs a little dog by my side.

Billy Graham once said, "I think God will have prepared everything for our perfect happiness. If it takes my dog being there (in Heaven), I believe he'll be there."[1] Billy and Ruth Graham loved their dogs. They had many throughout their lives. Billy

Are Max, Bella, and Jazz in Heaven?

once compared the virtue of dogs to how to be a better husband. "Dogs are quick to show their affection. They never pout; they never bear a grudge. They never run away from home when mistreated. They never complain about their food. They never gripe about the way the house is kept. They are chivalrous and courageous, ready to protect ... at the risk of their lives. They love children; no matter how noisy and boisterous they are, the dog loves every minute of it. Perhaps if we husbands imitated a few of our dog's virtues, life with our family might be more amiable."[2]

At the end of his life, Billy still had his faithful companion by his side. There's a portrait of him sitting in a rocking chair on the porch with his dog nearby. At 89, he tripped over his dog, sending Billy to the hospital. His doctor told him to continue to get exercise but be mindful of his dog.

Martin Luther had a dog, Tolpel (Clownie), that he loved very much. When asked if dogs are in Heaven, he said:

"Certainly, there will be, for Peter calls that day the time of the restitution of all things. Then, as is clearly said elsewhere, he will create a new heaven and a new earth. He will also create new Clownies with skin of gold and hair of pearls. There and then, God will be all in all. No animal will eat any other. Snakes and toads and other beasts which are poisonous on account of original sin will then be not only innocuous but even pleasing and nice to play with. Why is it that we cannot believe that all things will happen as the Bible says, even in this article about the resurrection? Original sin is at fault."[3]

And the one sitting on the throne said, "Look, I am making everything new!" And then he said to me, "Write this down, for what I tell you is trustworthy and true." (Revelation 21:5)

Everything. God does not lie. He is trustworthy. God is not going to start over from scratch. He is going to restore all that he created in the first place. Romans 8 speaks of the future glory in that ALL creation groans and waits for restoration.

> Yet what we suffer now is nothing compared to the glory he will reveal to us later. For all creation is waiting eagerly for that future day when God will reveal who his children really are. Against its will, all creation was subjected to God's curse. But with eager hope, the creation looks forward to the day when it will join God's children in glorious freedom from death and decay, for we know that all creation has been groaning as in the pains of childbirth right up to the present time. (Romans 8:18-22)

All creation--animals included.

Joni Eareckson Tata, paralyzed and in a wheelchair since her teens, wrote a beautiful book about Heaven.

"If God brings our pets back to life, it wouldn't surprise me. It would be just like Him. It would be totally in keeping with His generous character. . . . Exorbitant. Excessive. Extravagant in grace after grace. Of all the dazzling discoveries and ecstatic pleasures heaven will hold for us, the potential of seeing Scrappy would be pure whimsy—utterly, joyfully, surprisingly superfluous. . . . Heaven is going to be a place that will refract and reflect in as many ways as possible the goodness and joy of our great God, who delights in lavishing love on His children."[4]

> "Heaven is going to be a place that will refract and reflect in as many ways as possible the goodness and joy of our great God." JE

All through the Bible, God speaks of animals. Even before he created Adam and Eve, he made animals.

> Then God said, "Let the earth produce every sort of animal,

Are Max, Bella, and Jazz in Heaven?

each producing offspring of the same kind—livestock, small animals that scurry along the ground, and wild animals." And that is what happened. God made all sorts of wild animals, livestock, and small animals, each able to produce offspring of the same kind. And God saw that it was good. (Genesis 1:24, 25)

> The wolf and the lamb will feed together.

Isaiah lists animals on the New Earth two different times:

> In that day, the wolf and the lamb will live together; the leopard will lie down with the baby goat. The calf and the yearling will be safe with the lion, and a little child will lead them all. (Isaiah 11:6)

> "The wolf and the lamb will feed together. The lion will eat hay like a cow. But the snakes will eat dust. In those days, no one will be hurt or destroyed on my holy mountain. I, the LORD, have spoken!" (Isaiah 65:25)

Not sure I'm really into snakes on the New Earth.

Psalm 104 is a pictorial description of the New Earth. It describes providing water for all the animals and quenching the thirst of the donkey. The Psalmist pictures birds nesting in trees and singing among their branches, wild goats, badgers, young lions, and even large sea creatures.

> O Lord, what a variety of things you have made!
> In wisdom, you have made them all.
> The earth is full of your creatures.
> Here is the ocean, vast and wide,
> teeming with life of every kind,
> both large and small. (Psalm 104:24, 25)

The next part of this Psalm is fascinating.

They all depend on you
to give them food as they need it.
When you supply it, they gather it.
You open your hand to feed them,
and they are richly satisfied.
But if you turn away from them, they panic.
When you take away their breath,
they die and turn again to dust.
When you give them your breath, life is created,
and you renew the face of the earth. (Psalm 104:27-30)

I read this to say that there will come a time when God renews *all* on the face of the earth, animals included.

> God renews *ALL*.

Romans 8 says that "all creation groans and waits for the renewal of all things."

John Wesley, the father of the Methodist Church, loved animals, especially horses. He believed that one day God would restore all things, not just humankind. He advocated against cruelty to animals, especially those found in the gambling pits at the time. John spent his entire career on horseback, traveling from place to place. According to records, he rode 250,000 miles during his preaching career. He lovingly cared for each one of his horses, admonishing others to do the same. J. Tigert quoted him as saying: "Be merciful to your beast. Not only ride moderately, but see with your own eyes, that your horse be rubbed, fed, and bedded."[5] He even claimed that God healed his lame horse.

> "I took my leave of Newcastle, my horse was so exceedingly lame that I was afraid I must have lain by too. We could not discern what it was that was amiss, and yet he would scarce set his foot to the ground. After riding thus seven miles, I was thoroughly tired, and my head ached more than it had done for some months...I then thought, "Cannot God heal either man or beast, by any means or without any?" Immediately, my weariness

Are Max, Bella, and Jazz in Heaven?

and headache ceased, and my horse's lameness in the same instant. Nor did he halt anymore either that day or the next. A very odd accident this also!"[6]

Scriptures speak of horses throughout the Old and New Testaments. Remember Elijah? Angels escorted Elijah to Heaven in a chariot pulled by horses. As he and Elisha walked along, a fiery chariot and fiery horses suddenly appeared and separated them.

Elisha cried, "Oh, my father, my father! Israel's chariots and its riders" (2 Kings 2:12). What a way to go! Those horses are still in Heaven.

Revelation speaks of white, red, black, and green horses in Heaven (Revelation 6:2-8). Jesus rides the white horse in Revelation 19:11.

After reading *Black Beauty* and *My Friend Flicka*, many a little girl of my generation wanted a horse to call her own. I dreamed of owning a beautiful black horse with a white star on its forehead (that only I could ride). I finally got my horse when I turned sixteen. I didn't want a car; I just wanted a horse. I spent many happy hours riding my Pinto pony through the countryside. I can't wait to ride horses again on the New Earth. Perhaps I will finally own that beautiful black horse.

Are there talking animals on the New Earth? No? Maybe there are! I love the story of Balaam's donkey in Numbers 22. Balaam was a pagan prophet King Balak of Moab sent to curse the Israelites. "Please come and curse these people for me because they are too powerful. Then perhaps I will be able to conquer them and drive them from the land. I know that blessings fall on any people you bless, and curses fall on people you curse." God spoke to Balaam and told him not to go, but then God relented and said Balaam could go only if he spoke His words. God knew Balaam's heart, and that he probably wouldn't do as he asked, so God sent an angel to block his path. Balaam's donkey balked when he saw the angel. Angry, Balaam beat his donkey three different times until God gave the donkey the ability to speak.

Finally, God opened Balaam's eyes to see the angel. That

Talking animals?

poor donkey. Will animals talk on the New Earth? Who knows? But if God can open a donkey's mouth to speak on the Old Earth, why not? Listen in on this conversation in Numbers 22:28-30.

> "What have I done to you that deserves your beating me three times?" it asked Balaam.
>
> "You have made me look like a fool!" Balaam shouted. "If I had a sword with me, I would kill you!"
>
> "But I am the same donkey you have ridden all your life," the donkey answered. "Have I ever done anything like this before?"
>
> "No," Balaam admitted.

That brings up the question, do animals have souls? I read an interesting article from Eric Hernández, on his website, *Apologetics, Philosophy, Theology, and Engaging the Culture for the Truth of Christianity*. In reference to my question and the story of Balaam's donkey, he writes:

"As for a biblical basis, the word for soul is *nephesh*, and that word is used in Genesis when God creates animals and calls them nephesh, or "soulish" creatures. Also, seeing how they think and have free will would imply that they had a soul. The account of Balaam's donkey that spoke in the bible apparently had a stream of consciousness, and God opened his mouth to speak as the bible records in Numbers 22:28-30. There is no biblical objection to animals having souls. So given the philosophical argument from free will, consciousness, rationality, and the Hebrew word used in Genesis for the soul (nephesh), we can safely conclude that animals do, in fact, have souls, even if those souls do not have the same structure as ours."[7]

Interesting.

God charged Adam to name the animals (Genesis 2:19, 20). "He brought them to the man to see what he would call them,

Are Max, Bella, and Jazz in Heaven?

and the man chose a name for each one. He gave names to all the livestock, all the birds of the sky, and all the wild animals. But still there was no helper just right for him" (NLT). I think it's interesting that God created all these incredible creatures in the garden before he created Eve.

God preserved the animals during the Flood. He had a plan for them to replenish the earth. Why not the New Earth, also? In Deuteronomy 7:13, 14 and 28:1-4, God promises:

> He will love you and bless you, and he will give you many children. He will give fertility to your land and your animals. When you arrive in the land he swore to give your ancestors, you will have large harvests of grain, new wine, and olive oil, and great herds of cattle, sheep, and goats. You will be blessed above all the nations of the earth. None of your men or women will be childless, and all your livestock will bear young.

> If you fully obey the Lord your God and carefully keep all his commands that I am giving you today, the Lord your God will set you high above all the nations of the world. You will experience all these blessings if you obey the Lord your God:
> Your towns and your fields
> will be blessed.
> Your children and your crops
> will be blessed.
> The *offspring of your herds and flocks*
> will be blessed.
> Your fruit baskets and breadboards
> will be blessed.
> Wherever you go and whatever you do,
> you will be blessed.

These blessings and many more will carry over to the New Earth. Do they include animals? Yes, I absolutely think so. Are our sweet dogs in Heaven? I don't know. I do believe that God can restore them if he chooses. In the meantime, I will love and cherish the dogs I have now, hoping that someday on the New Earth, I will be surrounded by my beloved animals. Maybe, finally, Jazz will be able to happily chase that little rabbit down the streets of Jerusalem—never catching it, of course.

Are Max, Bella, and Jazz in Heaven?

Light-seeds

Paul wrote: "But with eager hope, the creation looks forward to the day when it will join God's children in glorious freedom from death and decay, for we know that all creation has been groaning as in the pains of childbirth right up to the present time." What does that say to you?

Martin Luther said: "Why is it that we cannot believe that all things will happen as the Bible says?" Do you believe all that the Bible says? Is that difficult for you?

I find this interesting: God created animals even before humans. Have you ever wondered why?

Psalm 27:30 says, "You *renew* the face of the earth." How do you read this?

So—will animals talk on the New Earth? (This is not a trick question.)

Joni Erekson wrote, "If God brings our pets back to life, it wouldn't surprise me. It would be just like Him. It would be totally in keeping with His generous character. . . . Exorbitant. Excessive. Extravagant in grace after grace." Is this your God?

Do the blessings of God carry over to the New Earth?

Walk Me Into Heaven

19

May We Sing for Joy to the End of Our Days or (In the Wait)

*Teach us to realize the brevity of life,
so that we may grow in wisdom.
O Lord, come back to us!
How long will you delay?
Take pity on your servants!
Satisfy us each morning with your unfailing love,
so we may sing for joy to the end of our lives.
(Psalm 90:12-14)*

Today is my birthday. I am 75 years old. I can hardly comprehend it as I sit and type that number. Interestingly, I have come to the end of my book on my birthday. It seems like just yesterday that I turned sixteen years old—and then, before I knew it, I was 40, and now I am 75. My joy has intensified, fueled by the Holy Spirit, as I have researched and read scriptures these last three months. Sometimes I have felt like a kid on Christmas Eve, so excited about God's promises, the Lord's Resurrection, and what that truly means for all eternity.

The Psalmist realized the importance of the brevity of life.

Walk Me Into Heaven

He longed for the Lord to come back and not delay, but in the wait, he asked that the Lord satisfy him daily with a love that could only fill him with joy until the end of his life. The KJV says this: "Teach us to number our days." At 75, I know that God has numbered my days. He knows how many days I have left before he walks me into Heaven. What do I do as I wait?

One sure thing, I don't want to sit on the porch in my spiritual "rocking chair" and wait until the Lord walks me into Heaven. I may not have the energy to go out into the world, but that doesn't mean God cannot use me in other ways. In chapter two, I wrote about all the saints before us whom the Lord has used even until the end of their days.

> And I am certain that God, who began the good work within you, will continue his work until it is finally finished on the day when Christ Jesus returns. (Philippians 1:6)

John R. Rice (1895-1980), an influential Baptist evangelist of his time, wrote these words:

> "We [wrongly] feel that Heaven is bearable, all right, when one has sucked dry all the pleasures of earth. We feel that, only after old age has come upon us, when life is a burden, when health has failed, when we are in the way and our children don't want us, then perhaps we should be resigned to go to Heaven. Subconsciously we look upon Heaven as a scrap heap for the worn-out and useless, a kind of old people's home – better than nothing but not as good as this world, with youth, health, and prosperity."[1]

I don't want to be "sucked dry" here on earth and sent to the heavenly old folks' home! I hope that God will continue to use my life to further his kingdom. Someone once asked Billy Graham if the purpose of salvation was to be with Jesus, why would he leave us here on earth? He said: "Earth isn't just Heaven's waiting room where we sit around doing nothing; earth is the stage on which the drama of the ages is being played out. It demonstrates Christ's victory over sin, death, Hell, and Satan. And no matter who we are, we have a God-given role to play in that divine drama."[2]

Don't you hate waiting rooms? What a waste of time! As we get older, we spend a lot of time in doctors' waiting rooms. We wait when we get to the office, and then we wait when we get into the examining room. My Uncle Wayne did not like to wait. One day at the doctor's office, he was all dressed in his examination gown, and after a while, he got tired of the wait. He slipped off the examining table, opened the door, walked out into the hall, and announced to all within earshot, "I'm here! Are you there?" I laugh just thinking about Uncle Wayne standing in the hall in his short little gown.

Waiting on Heaven doesn't have to be that way.

If we're willing, he keeps us front and center, filling us with his Spirit to continue to work for his kingdom.

> My response is to get down on my knees before the Father, this magnificent Father who parcels out all Heaven and earth. I ask him to strengthen us by his Spirit—not a brute strength but a glorious inner strength—that Christ will live in us as we open the door and invite him in. And I ask him that with both feet planted firmly on love, we'll be able to take in with all followers of Jesus the extravagant dimensions of Christ's love. Reach out and experience the breadth! Test its length! Plumb the depths! Rise to the heights! Live full lives, full in the fullness of God.
>
> God can do anything, you know—far more than we could ever imagine or guess or request in our wildest dreams! He does it not by pushing us around but by working within us, his Spirit deeply and gently within us. (Ephesians 3:14-19, Message)

Even at 55, 75, or even 95, our spirit man and woman have no retirement plan, age limit, or restriction. "God can do anything, you know." The key is "if we're willing." God will never give up on us during the wait. He will use us in ways we can't even imagine. As we wait for the Lord's coming or our time to go to be with him, "Be patient as you wait for the Lord's return. Consider the farmers who patiently wait for the rains in the fall and in the spring. They eagerly look for the valuable harvest to ripen. You, too, must be patient. Take courage, for the coming of the Lord is near" (James 5:7, 8).

There used to be a popular expression on a kid's T-shirt: "Don't give up on me; God's not finished with me yet." The same goes for old age.

> Even when I am old and gray,
> do not forsake me, my God,
> till I declare your power to the next generation,
> your mighty acts to all who are to come. (Psalm 71:18, NIV)

If we plop down in our spiritual rocking chair and let the world go by, we will miss many unique opportunities for God to work through us, even in small ways. God will not be finished with us on earth until we step foot with him in Heaven. In the meantime, he has work for us to do. My good friend, Mary Jo Bevis, taught our women's Bible Study until she was 90. She continued after that to teach her beloved Sunday School class. There was no spiritual rocking chair for Mrs. Mary Jo.

It must be more and more difficult waiting on God as we grow into our 80s and 90s. Friends, family members, and others begin to leave us and make their way into Heaven. Many 90-year-old saints are the last of their family

> God does not stick us away in a room alone or even in a spiritual old folks' home and leave us there.

and friends. My grandmother died at 103—no one left in her town to remember her life except for her beloved family. We buried her on a cold autumn day beside her cherished husband and her son, my daddy. Huddled under a tent at her graveside, we shared our memories of Grandmother. She would have been pleased.

184

May We Sing for Joy to the End of Our Days

I love the story of Bertha, a 95-year-old woman, in a nursing home. A church lady came to see her and asked how she was doing. Bertha told her that she was just worried sick. Concerned, the church lady asked if they were taking good care of her. "Yes, they are wonderful to me here." The visitor asked if she was in pain. "No, I'm feeling fit as a fiddle!" Curious, the church lady said, "Well, what are you worried about?" Bertha leaned forward in her rocking chair and said, "Honey, all my dear friends have already died and gone to Heaven. I'm worried that they're wondering where I went!"

As I come to the end of this book, I think about Paul. He experienced a taste of Heaven. While he waited in prison, don't you know he yearned for its freedom? But he knew that God wasn't finished with him yet. He wrote these words in Philippians 1:20-26:

> For I fully expect and hope that I will never be ashamed, but that I will continue to be bold for Christ, as I have been in the past. And I trust that my life will bring honor to Christ, whether I live or die. For to me, living means living for Christ, and dying is even better. But if I live, I can do more fruitful work for Christ. So, I really don't know which is better. I'm torn between two desires: I long to go and be with Christ, which would be far better for me. But for your sakes, it is better that I continue to live.
>
> Knowing this, I am convinced that I will remain alive so I can continue to help all of you grow and experience the joy of your faith. And when I come to you again, you will have even more reason to take pride in Christ Jesus because of what he is doing through me.

Only God knows the date that he will walk me into Heaven. It's fun to dream of what that will be like. In the meantime, in the wait, I can confidently trust that he orders each one of my days until then.

The Lord directs the steps of the godly.

Walk Me Into Heaven

He delights in every detail of their lives.
Though they stumble, they will never fall,
for the Lord holds them by the hand.
Once I was young, and now I am old.
Yet I have never seen the godly abandoned
or their children begging for bread. (Psalm 37: 23-25)

At the end of his life, with his family at his bedside, Dwight L. Moody said aloud: "Earth recedes, and heaven opens before me. If this is death, there is nothing awful here. It is sweet. This is bliss. Do not call me back. God is calling me. I must go. There is no valley here. It is all beautiful."[3] And he died a brief time later, on Dec. 26, 1899.

124 years later, Tim Keller, beloved pastor and author, died recently after a long battle with pancreatic cancer. He left these words for his children, "There is no downside for me leaving, not in the slightest. See you soon, Dad."

This is what we long for, why Jesus came to earth, and why the resurrection is so important. We will someday reunite with our loved ones—those who know Jesus as their Lord. God will call our name, give us a hand, and joyfully walk us into Heaven. It is all beautiful.

I stretch forth my hands unto thee:
My soul thirsteth after thee, as a thirsty land.
(Psalm 143:6, KJV)

Soli Deo Gloria

Light-seeds

Teach us to number our days (Psalm 90:12). How do you do that?

How will God continue the good work in you?

Have you ever thought about Heaven as the scrap heap for the worn-out and useless?

Billy Graham said, "Earth isn't Heaven's waiting room, where we sit around doing nothing until it's time to depart. We have a God-given role to play in the divine drama." What is your role?

"God can do anything, you know." How can he use you in the wait?

Walk Me Into Heaven

End Notes

Introduction
1. *It Is Well With My Soul*, Lyrics by Horatio Spafford and Music by Philip Bliss, 1876.
2. *Abide With Me*, Written by Henry Francis Lyte in 1847 as he was dying from tuberculosis.
3. *In the Sweet By and By*, Written by Joseph P. Webster, 1868.
4. Moody, D. L. (1900). *Heaven*. The Moody Press, Chicago, Illinois. (https://www.preceptaustin.org/heaven_-_d_l_moody).
5. Alcorn, R. (2014). *Heaven*. Tyndale Press.
6. Randy Alcorn, (March 28, 2022) by Twitter, (https://twitter.com/randyalcorn/status/1508573678086230016), March 28, 2022.

Chapter One—Before We Begin to Talk About Heaven
1. Holy Bible, *New Living Translation*. Tyndale House Publishers (Original work published 1996). The Holy Bible, New International Version. (1984).
2. Peterson, E. (1993). *The Message Bible*. NavPress.
3. Institute for Bible Reading (2009). *Immerse: The Reading Bible*. Tyndale House Publishers.
4. (2015). *YouVersion* (Version 8.23, RED 2.10. 1.2272) [Mobile

app].
5. Warner Sallman. (2023, April 7). In *Wikipedia*.https://en.wikipedia.-org/wiki/Warner_Sallman

Chapter Two—Getting Old is Heck
1. Willard, D. (1997). *The Divine Conspiracy*. HarperOne.
2. Twain, M. (2015). *Bite-Size Twain: Wit and Wisdom from the Literary Legend* (p. 29). St. Martin's Press.
3. *Fame* (Irene Cara song). (2023, April 8). In *Wikipedia*. https://en.wikipedia.org/wiki/Fame_(Irene_Cara_song)
4. Graham, B. (2011). *Nearing Home: Life, Faith, and Finishing Well*. Thomas Nelson.
5. McCinnes, A. (2022, February 14). *The Church Is Losing Its Grayheads*. Christianity Today. Retrieved November 8, 2022, from https://www.christianitytoday.com/ct/2022/march/gray-gen-x-boomers-older-churchgoers-leaving-church.html
6. (2011, May 26). *Barna Describes Religious Changes Among Busters, Boomers, and Elders Since 1991*. Barna. Retrieved November 10, 2022, from https://www.barna.com/research/barna-describes-religious-changes-among-busters-boomers-and-elders-since-1991/

Chapter Three—The Courage to Get to the End
1. Charles Studd. (2023, May 1). In *Wikipedia*. https://en.wikipedia.org/wiki/Charles_Studd
2. Owens, T. (n.d.). *Walking Through the Fire*. World Magazine. Retrieved November 20, 2022, from https://www.wng.org/articles/walking-through-fire-1617326251
3. Saint, S. (2015, June 15). *Tribute to Aunt Betty*. Facebook. Retrieved November 24, 2022, from https://m.facebook.com/ITEC.USA/photos-/a.10150394298073066/10153920033923066/?-type=3.

Chapter Four—College Hunks Hauling Junk
1. College Hunks Hauling Junk ® www.collegehunkshaulingjunk.com.

Endnotes

2. Gill, S. (2018, January 5). *Your Kids Don't Want to Inherit Your Clutter, A professional organizer we love offers 5 steps to streamlining your stuff — So your family won't have to.* Modern Loss. Retrieved November 28, 2022, from https://modernloss.com/your-kids-dont-want-to-inherit-your-clutter/
3. Elgato Video Capture, https://www.elgato.com/en/video-capture.
4. Joiner, S. (2022, July 22). *Common Questions About Estate Planning: Answered.* Maumellelaw.com. Retrieved November 28, 2022, from https://www.maumellelaw.com/common-questions-about-estate-planning-answered
5. Jones, J. M. (1, June 23). *How Many Americans Have A Will?* Gallup. Retrieved November 28, 2022, from https://news.gallup.com/poll/351500/how-many-americans-have-will.aspx
6. Widness, B. (2012, May 23). *10 Things You Should Know About Writing A Will.* AARP. Retrieved November 28, 2022, from https://www.aarp.org/money/estate-planning/info-09-2010/ten_things_you_should_know_about_writing_a_will.html
7. Hayyei, S. (2019, November 22). *A Family Reconciles.* JTS.edu. Retrieved November 30, 2022, from https://www.jtsa.edu/torah/a-family-reconciles/
8. Earl, C. G. (7, January 1). *Discussing Your Medical Wishes: A Patient's Guide.* Focus On The Family.com. Retrieved November 30, 2022, from https://www.focusonthefamily.com/pro-life/discussing-your-medical-wishes-a-patients-guide/
9. Five Wishes (n.d.). FiveWishes.org. Retrieved November 30, 2022, from https://www.fivewishes.org

Chapter Five—Traveling Toward Heaven

1. Hannon, S. (2023, May 21). *Risen: Jesus Appeared to the Disciples* [Sermon]. Fellowship Bible Church, NWA. https://www.fellowshipnwa.org/teaching/7404?service=773
2. Nancy, O. (2016, October 18). *What Do Muslims Believe?* Christianitytoday.com. Retrieved December 6, 2022, from https://www.christianitytoday.com/biblestudies/articles/evangelism/what-do-muslims-believe.html

3. Elliot, E. (2021). *All That Was Ever Ours*. Baker Books.

Chapter Six—The Spectators
1. I read this quote several years ago. The source is www.sacredspace.ie. (2013) I don't know the author.
2. Rice, J. R. (1940). *Bible Facts About Heaven* (p. 38). Sword of the Lord.
3. Hamilton, C. L. (2013). *To See Him Face to Face*. Xulon Press.

Chapter Seven—The Hard Chapter
1. E, J. (1883). *The Voice of Wisdom: A Treasury of Moral Truths from the Best Authors* (p. 71). William P. Nimmo & Co.
2. Lewis, C. S. (2016). *The Complete C.S. Lewis Signature Classics: The Problem of Pain* (p. 416). San Francisco: HarperSanFrancisco.
3. Keller, T. (2021, May 21). *Tweet*. Twitter. Retrieved December 12, 2022, from https://twitter.com/timkellernyc/status/1395744695570083843?lang=en
4. Edwards, J. (1771, May 8). *Sinners in the Hand of an Angry God*. Christian Classics Ethereal Library. Retrieved December 15, 2022, from https://ccel.org/ccel/edwards/sermons.sinners.html
5. A. W. Tozer, *God Tells the Man Who Cares* (Camp Hill, PA: WingSpread, 1992), p. 39.
6. Packer, J. L. (1993). *Knowing God* (pp. 143, 147). Downers Grove, IL: InterVarsity Press.
7. Lewine, S. A. (2022, April 19). *God's View of Equality and Equity*. The Way of the Word. Retrieved December 29, 2022, from https://sheilaalewine.com/2022/04/19/gods-view-of-equality-equity/
8. Graham, B. (2012, October 23). *Answers*. Billygraham.org. Retrieved December 29, 2022, from https://billygraham.org/answer/i-heard-someone-say-the-other-day-that-when-we-get-to-heaven-were-probably-going-to-be-surprised-at-some-of-the-people-who-will-be-there/
9. Beggs, A. (2019, November 20). *The Power and Message of*

the Cross [Sermon]. Truthforlife.org. https://www.youtube.com/watch?v=SL8mJQ39zjw&t=0s

Home
1. Graham, B. (2021). *Who's in Charge of a World That Suffers?* (p. 202). Thomas Nelson.

Chapter Eight—"Good News, Silas! You Were Right!"
1. Moody, D. L. (1900). *Heaven*. The Moody Press, Chicago, Illinois. https://www.preceptaustin.org/heaven_-_d_l_moody.
2. Shriver, M. (2007). *What's Heaven* (1st ed.). Golden Books Adult Publishing.
3. Wright, N. T. (2019, December 6). *Christians Wrong About Heaven*. Time.com. Retrieved December 30, 2022, from https://time.com/5743505/new-testament-heaven/
4. Eldridge, J. (2018). *All Things New: Heaven, Earth, and the Restoration of Everything You Love*. Thomas Nelson.

Chapter Nine—Sore Puzzler
1. Alcorn, R. (2020, April 3). *What Are My Loved Ones Experiencing in the Present Heaven?* Epm.org. Retrieved January 5, 2023, from https://www.epm.org/blog/2020/Jun/3/loved-ones-experiencing-heaven
2. Jeffress, R. (2019, September 5). *The Present Heaven and the Future Heaven*. Ptv.org. Retrieved January 5, 2023, from https://ptv.org/devotional/the-present-heaven-and-the-future-heaven/ (This linke does not work anymore.)
3. Moody, R. A. (1976). *Life After Life*. Mockingbird Books.
4. Moody, R. A. (1977). *Reflections on Life After Life*. Stackpole Books.
5. Hayasaki, E. (2014). *The Death Class: A True Story about Life* (pp. 11-12). New York: Simon and Schuster.
6. Zigarelli, M. (2022, August 9). *Another Way In: "Near-Death Experiences" as an Apologetic*. Christian Scholars Review. https://christianscholars.com/another-way-in-near-death-experiences-as-an-apologetic/

Chapter Ten—Yearning to Be at Home With the Lord
1. (1927, September 27). *The Mystery Woman, Lillian Ailing.* Whitehorsestar.com. https://www.whitehorsestar.com/History/the-mystery-woman-lillian-ailing-part-1-0f-3
2. Dickie, Francis (March–April 1972). "Mysterious Lillian — Human Homing Pigeon". *True West.* Vol. 19, no. 4. Austin, Texas: Western Publications, Inc. pp. 12–15, 55–56.
3. Pybus, C. (2002). *The Woman Who Walked to Russia: A writer's search for a lost legend.* New York, New York: Four Walls Eight Windows.
4. Alcorn, R. (2020, June 3). *What Are My Loved Ones Experiencing in the Present Heaven?* Epm.org. Retrieved January 16, 2023, from https://www.epm.org/blog/2020/-Jun/3/loved-ones-experiencing-heaven
5. Gruden, W. *Systematic Theology.* Copyright © 1994 by Wayne Grudem. Appendix 6 and glossary copyright © 2000 by Wayne Grudem. This book is published jointly by Inter-Varsity Press, 38 De Montfort Street, Leicester LE1 7GP, Great Britain, and by Zondervan Publishing House, 5300 Patterson Avenue S.E., Grand Rapids, Michigan, USA.
6. Rice, J. R. (1940). *Bible Facts About Heaven* (p. 15). Sword of the Lord.

Chapter Eleven—"Look! I Am Making All Things New!"
1. Alcorn, R. (2004). *Heaven* (p.154). Tyndale House.
2. Hoekema, A. A. (1994). *The Bible and the Future.* United States: Wm. B. Eerdmans Publishing Company.
3. Leuke, P. (n.d.). *What Are the New Heaven and the New Earth?* Lifehopeandtruth.com. Retrieved January 20, 2023, from https://lifehopeandtruth.com/prophecy/revelation/new-heavens-and-new-earth/
4. Andress, B. (2016, November 7). *A New Earth or A Renewed Earth?* Christianweek.org. Retrieved January 21, 2023, from https://www.christianweek.org/new-earth-renewed-earth/
5. Stevenson, Gregory (2013) *The Theology of Creation in the*

Endnotes

Book of Revelation, Leaven: Vol. 21: Iss. 3, Article 6.

Chapter Twelve—Spending Forever Time With the Lord
1. Hamilton, C. (2013). *To See Him Face to Face* (p. 128). Self-Published.
2. Ibid, p. 184
3. Riddle, JL (2009). *Revelation Song* © was written by Jennie Lee Riddle, Performed by Phillips, Craig & Dean on their album, Fearless.
4. McArthur, J. (1997). *The Glory of Heaven: The Truth about Heaven, Angels, and Eternal Life* (2nd ed., p. 110). Crossway.

Chapter Thirteen—The Holy City--the New Jerusalem
1. Alcorn, R. (2004). *Heaven* (p. 249). Tyndale House.
2. Elliott, C. J. (1905, January 1). *Commentary on Revelations 21.* Studylight.org. Retrieved January 22, 2023, from https://www.studylight.org/commentaries/eng/ebc/revelation-21.html
3. Alcorn, R. (2004). *Heaven* (p.251). Tyndale House
4. Moody, D. L. (1884, January 1). *Heaven: Where it Is, Its Inhabitants, and How to Get There.* Google.com. Retrieved January 23, 2023, from https://www.google.com-/books/edition/Heaven/sxhLAQAAMAAJ?hl=en&gbpv=0

Chapter Fourteen—I Can Only Imagine
1. *I Can Only Imagine* ©, written and composed by Bart Millard and performed by *Mercy Me,* 1999.
2. Moody, D. L. (1884, January 1). *Heaven: Where it Is, Its Inhabitants, and how to Get There.* Google.com. Retrieved January 23, 2023, from https://www.google.com-/books/edition/Heaven/sxhLAQAAMAAJ?hl=en&gbpv=0
3. Buechner, F. (1993). *Whistling in the Dark: An ABC Theologized* (p. 59). Harper and Row.
4. Black, D. (2010). *Flight to Heaven: A Plane Crash...A Lone Survivor...A Journey to Heaven . . . .*(p. 99). Bethany House.

Chapter Fifteen—What's There to Do Forever and Ever and Ever

1. Tozer, A. W.. Worship: *The Reason We Were Created-Collected Insights from A. W. Tozer*. United States, Moody Publishers, 2017.
2. Graham, B. (2017, May 10). *Answers*. Billygraham.org. Retrieved January 20, 2023, from https://billygraham.org/answer/will-we-get-bored-in-heaven/
3. Alcorn, R. (2017, September 26). *No More Boredom*. Patheos.com. Retrieved January 21, 2023, from https://www.patheos.com/blogs/randyalcorn/2017/09/no-more-boredom/
4. Brown, D. J. (2016, April 15). *Say Goodbye to Your Bucket List*. Fromthestudy.com. Retrieved January 23, 2023, from https://fromthestudy.com/2016/04/15/say-goodbye-to-your-bucket-list/
5. McArthur, J. (1987, October 25). *What Heaven Is*. Gty.org. Retrieved January 28, 2023, from https://www.gty.org/library/sermons-library/90-12/what-heaven-is
6. Costner, K. (Director). (2022). *Yellowstone 150* [Film]. Warm Springs Productions.
7. Alcorn, R. (2015, March 4). *Why the Reality of the Resurrection Means You Don't Need a "Bucket List"*. Epm.org. Retrieved January 27, 2023, from https://www.epm.org/blog/2015/Mar/4/resurrection-bucket-list
8. *The Lord of the Dance* ©, (1960) written by Sydney Carter. The melody is taken from an old Shaker song, *Simple Gifts*.
9. Hoekema, A. (2003, June 1). *Heaven: Not Just An Eternal Day Off*. Christianitytoday.com. Retrieved January 29, 2023, from https://www.christianitytoday.com/ct/2003/junewebonly/6-2-54.0.html

Chapter Sixteen—(RIP) Rest in Peace? or (WIP) Work in Peace?
1. Hamilton, C. (2013, November 5). *Heaven*. Cindy--experiencingthelight.Blogspot.com. Retrieved January 29, 2023, from https://cindy--experiencingthelight.blogspot.com-/2013/11/heaven.html
2. Anonymous (1905, January 1). *A Tired Housewife*. Interestingliterature.com. Retrieved January 30, 2023, from https://

Endnotes

interestingliterature.com/2019/01/on-a-tired-housewife-an-anonymous-poem/
3. (n.d.). *Will We Work/Have Jobs in Heaven?* Gotquestions.org. Retrieved February 3, 2023, from https://www.gotquestions.org/work-in-heaven.html
4. Burdette, J. J. (1922, April 8). Beyond the Sunset. *The Baptist, Volume 3*, p. 299.
5. *Sermons Preached in 1883 [to] 1887, Volume 18* (p. 141). Funk & Wagnalls. https://www.google.com/books/edition/Sermons_Preached_in_1883_to_1887/ZcpaAAAAYAAJ?hl=en&gbpv=0
6. Pease, G. (2014) quotes W.A Criswell. *Occupations in Heaven*. Sermons.Logos.Come. Retrieved February 12, 2023, from https://sermons.logos.com/sermons/124758-occupations-in-heaven
7. Gregg, D. (1872). *The Heaven Life or Stimulus for Two Worlds* (p. 62). Harvard University. https://www.google.com/books/edition/The_Heaven_life/D-oQAAAAYAAJ?hl=en&gbpv=0

Chapter Seventeen—It's Resurrection, Resurrection, Always Resurrection
1. Angelo, M. (n.d.). *How Chuck Colson's Legacy of Hope Lives On*. Prisonfellowship.org. Retrieved February 16, 2023, from https://www.prisonfellowship.org/2018/04/chuck-colsons-legacy-hope-lives/
2. Frazee, R. (2017). *What Happens After You Die: A Biblical Guide to Paradise, Hell and Life After Death* (p. 107). Thomas Nelson.
3. Spurgeon, C. H. (1859). *Spurgeon's Sermons Volume 5: The Wounds of Jesus* (p. 204). Devoted Publishing.
4. Hamilton, C. L. (2021). *To See Him Face to Face* (2nd ed., pp. 60, 61). Self-Published.

Chapter Eighteen—Are Max, Bella, and Jazz in Heaven?
1. Graham, B. (n.d.). *Will There Be Animals in Heaven?* Bil-

lygraham.org.uk. Retrieved February 15, 2024, from https://billygraham.org.uk/answer/i-suppose-youve-been-asked-this-before-but-will-there-be-animals-in-heaven/)
2. Graham, B. (2014, June 18). *Dog Virtues*. Billygrahamlibrary.org. Retrieved February 15, 2024, from https://billygrahamlibrary.org/wit-wisdom-the-love-of-dogs/
3. Martin Luther, from Preserved Smith, *The Life and Letters of Martin Luther*, (London: John Murray, 1911) p. 362.]
4. Tada, J. E. (1999). *Holiness in Hidden Places*. Thomas Nelson Incorporated.
5. Tigert, J. J. (1870). *A Constitutional History of American Episcopal Methodism* (p. 567). University of Georgia Libraries.
6. Wesley, J. (2019). *The Heart of John Wesley's Journal* (p. 138). Eaton & Mains.
7. Hernandez, E. (2014, December 12). Question #9 Do animals have souls? Eric Hernandez Ministries Apologetics, Philosophy, Theology, and Engaging the Culture for the Truth of Christianity. http://www.erichernandezministries.com/question-9-do-animals-have-souls/

Chapter Nineteen—May We Sing for Joy to the Ned of Our Lives
1. Rice, J. R. (1940). *Bible Facts About Heaven* (p. 38). Sword of the Lord.
2. Graham, B. (2021, December 12). *Answers*. Billygraham.org. Retrieved February 24, 2023, from https://billygraham.org/answer/why-do-we-have-to-wait-for-heaven/
3. Moody, D. L. (1900). *Echoes from the Pulpit and Platform* (p. 110). A.D. Worthington.

About the Author

Cindy Hamilton's passion is God, family, and friends. Her joy is complete in the presence of God, reading his Word and teaching from her heart. God has given her an imagination that takes the Bible and opens it up for others in a fun and practical way. She is a wife, mother to three amazing adults, mother-in-law to an incredible daughter-in-law, two great sons-in-law, "Cisa" to her beloved grandchildren, Bible study teacher, retired school counselor, and cancer survivor. She lives with her husband, Preston, in the small farming community of Lonoke, Arkansas.

She has self-published two books: *To See Him Face to Face* (2003), a book of stories from the New Testament written in the first person and *Anna's Chair* (2018). This fictional book is inspired by a family of missionaries who escaped civil war in Malakal, South Sudan, in 2011. After writing *Anna's Chair*, she was blessed to meet this family and now serves on the Board of Directors of their ministry, Gather1.

Walk Me Into Heaven

Endnotes

Desclaimer

Dear Reader,

So . . . I understand it is not a "best practice" to insert exclamation points in my writing, leaving readers to place their own. As I was writing this book, I couldn't help myself. In writing about Heaven and the afterlife, I would get so caught up in the thrill of the future that the exclamation points just had to be there.

Thanks for giving me grace! (Last one, I promise.)

Cindy

Walk Me Into Heaven

Endnotes

Made in the USA
Columbia, SC
15 August 2024